Endorsements for Russ Crosson and
8 Important Money Decisions for Every Couple

"Having been in the communications business nearly 30 years and married for nearly 25 of those years, I was excited to see a book on the subject of money that is really as much about communication as it is about money. Russ Crosson covers both subjects with precision and discernment, reminding me I must never stop learning about money or communication. Every couple should study this book together."

Mark DeMoss, founder,
The DeMoss Group

"I thoroughly enjoy Russ Crosson's rich and credible financial counsel in this book. It equips and empowers a couple to live in harmony, free from financial bondage."

Karen Loritts,
Conference speaker

"There are key decisions that every couple makes when it comes to money that determine long-term direction and destination. However, men and women communicate differently and have different perspectives when it comes to money. I wholeheartedly endorse this book by Russ Crosson. It not only gives practical advice for eight important financial areas every couple must address, but it also takes the stress out of the discussion, ultimately leading to more unity, harmony, and peace of mind for couples."

Mark Batterson, author of *The Circle Maker*, and
lead pastor, National Community Church

"We all know that one of the most common sources of conflict in any marriage is money. We also know that money issues are not primarily about money. As Jesus indicates, money is a revealer of the heart. In this book, Russ Crosson gets to the heart of the matter. I have known Russ and Julie for nearly 30 years. I have not only been blessed by their teaching but also by their friendship. I can truly say that the content of this book is born out of their own lives and marriage. I have seen them practice what they preach. I believe that every married (or soon-to-be-married) couple will benefit greatly by the biblical insights and practical wisdom found in *8 Important Money Decisions for Every Couple*."

Tim Kallam, senior pastor,
Mountain Brook Community Church

8 Important MONEY Decisions
for Every Couple

RUSS CROSSON

HARVEST HOUSE PUBLISHERS
EUGENE, OREGON

Cover design by Koechel Peterson & Associates, Inc., Minneapolis, Minnesota

Russ Crosson is published in association with the literary agency of Wolgemuth & Associates, Inc.

8 IMPORTANT MONEY DECISIONS FOR EVERY COUPLE

Copyright © 1989; updated edition © 2012 by Russell D. Crosson
Published 2012 by Harvest House Publishers
Eugene, Oregon 97402
www.harvesthousepublishers.com

Library of Congress Cataloging-in-Publication Data

Crosson, Russ
  Eight important money decisions for every couple / Russ Crosson.
    p. cm.
  Includes bibliographical references.
  ISBN 978-0-7369-4622-3 (pbk.)
  ISBN 978-0-7369-4623-0 (eBook)
  1. Married people—Finance, Personal. 2. Christians—Finance, Personal. 3. Finance, Personal—Religious aspects—Christianity. I. Title.
  HG179.C7497 2013
  332.024—dc23
                                                                    2011048661

*To all couples
who desire to make money
a nonissue in their marriages.*

Acknowledgments

To write a book on marital harmony and money management is indeed a challenge, and one that would be impossible for me were it not for my relationship with *Julie,* my bride of more than 30 years. Her love for God and unwavering desire to be a godly "helper" have enabled us, as a couple, to live out firsthand the financial principles and thoughts shared throughout this book. I'm extremely grateful for her and her constant support and encouragement. I am committed to her for the rest of my life. We are both grateful for the saving work Christ has done in our lives, without which the power and ability to live out these truths would be impossible.

I owe a special debt of gratitude to *Charles and Peggy McCreight,* who, along with the young couples in their church in Sumter, South Carolina, provided the forum where this material originally came together. Charles and Peggy encouraged Julie and me. They prayed for us constantly as we undertook the challenge of this project.

Ron Blue gave me the opportunity to work with couples in the financial arena when he hired me more than three decades ago. Financial insights gleaned from Ron, as well as my other partners at Ronald Blue & Company, are woven throughout this book. I am grateful these people are in my life.

The couples who read the manuscript and offered valuable input have had a tremendous impact on the finished product. *Rusty and Colleen Reid, Baker and Vicky Jones, Clark and Holly Crosson,* and *Reed and Kristen Crosson* deserve my special thanks.

To Julie's and my parents, *Bert and Jan Harned* and *Lon Dean and Barbara Crosson*—Julie and I are forever grateful for their presence in our lives. They modeled harmonious marriages and the proper way to handle finances for us. They have been an inspiration to us.

A special thanks to *Bonnie Davidson* and *Molly Blass* for their countless hours of inputting and responding to my time demands as this book came to completion.

Contents

Foreword by Dennis Rainey, CEO
and cofounder of FamilyLife 9

Introduction 11

PART 1: THE FOUNDATION

1. The Purpose of Money 23

2. The Purpose of Marriage 35

3. Reasons for Marriage Conflict 51

4. Work: Blessing or Curse? 67

PART 2: 8 IMPORTANT DECISIONS

5. Will He Ever Come Home? 79
    Decision 1: *How Much Should We Work?*

6. The Myth of the Working Mother 89
    Decision 2: *Should Mom Work Outside the Home?*

7. The Checkbook 103
    Decision 3: *Who Pays the Bills?*

8. Freedom in Control 119
    Decision 4: *How Do We Set Budget Amounts?*

9. The Banker Is Calling 133
    Decision 5: *How Much Debt Should We Allow?*

10. But It's Such a Good Deal! 147
    Decision 6: *How Do We Decide Which Investments
    to Make?*

11. To Give or Not to Give 163
    Decision 7: *How Much Should We Give?*

12. A Game Plan for Communication 171
    Decision 8: *What Is Our Strategy for Discussing Money?*

13. A Woman's Perspective on Her God-Given Roles 189
    Julie Crosson's Personal Story

The Ultimate Power Source 205

Recommended Resources 209

Living Expenses Worksheet 211

Notes 213

Foreword

by Dennis Rainey,
CEO and cofounder of FamilyLife

As part of the most famous address ever given on planet Earth, Jesus Christ taught about the importance of how we treat money:

> Do not lay up for yourselves treasures on earth, where moth and rust destroy and where thieves break in and steal, but lay up for yourselves treasures in heaven, where neither moth nor rust destroys and where thieves do not break in and steal. For where your treasure is, there your heart will be also...No one can serve two masters, for either he will hate the one and love the other, or he will be devoted to the one and despise the other. You cannot serve God and money (Matthew 6:19-20,24 ESV).

Jesus warns us that our use of money is a reflection of what we value and what we're living for. It's no wonder that the use of money can reveal so many differences and create so much conflict in a marriage. Enter Russ Crosson to offer help and hope as you deal with money within your marriage. You've made a great decision in choosing this book because the "right man" has written it. Let me explain.

Every book is a reflection of the worldview of its author. Russ's worldview transcends cultures and trends because it is based on the Scriptures. As a result, he's the right man to address how a couple handles money because he has the right foundation for his worldview, resulting in the right convictions about money.

My experience in working with couples for nearly four decades tells me that couples starting out in marriage today are in need of training about how to approach the issue of money. Most of these people seem to be biblically illiterate. As a result, they take their marching orders from the culture they live in. Russ gets this. He understands that if a husband and wife are going to experience harmony in their marriage, they must "sing off the same song sheet." He also understands that every couple needs convictions about money from a source they can trust, and he patiently instructs couples from the bestselling book of all time—the Bible.

Professionally, Russ is also the right man because he has the right experience and education. This book is the sage wisdom from a man who has waded into the deep waters of finances with hundreds of couples. Since 1980, Russ has interacted with couples about their money—how they view it, invest it, spend it, save it, and give it. As a result, his perspective and counsel exceeds that of even the most prestigious finance gurus. So when Russ exhorts a married couple that there are eight important money decisions they must make, you can trust him. I encourage you to listen to him!

Finally, Russ is the right man because he is a man of integrity. He has the right character that results in the right model. Russ isn't perfect, but he is a mature follower of Christ. I've checked Russ out, and he is worthy of emulating. I've never heard a negative word about him. That's pretty amazing when I consider that he's helped so many people with something that's important to them—their money.

I hope you and your spouse will read this book as a couple. I suggest you consider finding an older couple to go through it with you and mentor you. Then I implore you to do the hard work of applying the principles. I promise you, although it will be hard work, the rewards are both now and eternal.

After a few years of making these important and right money decisions, you'll experience a track record of freedom and real success. Then I encourage you to consider reaching out to a newly married couple and offering to mentor them in this important area. If you do, you will truly be prosperous as a couple.

Dennis Rainey

Introduction

Let's imagine that nestled in the lush Green Mountains of Vermont is a quaint bed-and-breakfast known as Village Crest Inn. Besides award-winning food and breathtaking views of Pico Peak, this inn boasts a very unique tagline: "The best place to plan the rest of your life!"

Village Crest Inn is operated by John and Dottie Finch, an energetic couple in their late fifties who love to help couples strengthen their marriages. John and Dottie held high-profile jobs when they met at the corporate headquarters of a telecommunications company. Dottie was an organizational designer who created engaging, adult-learning workshops. John was a recruiter who worked in Human Resources. His claim to fame was that he really knew how to read people.

When accounting scandals and buyouts plagued the communications industry, the Finches decided to get off the corporate treadmill. They sold their plush Virginia home, cashed in their stocks, and headed to Vermont to build a new life. When they stumbled onto the grounds of Village Crest, they found a home where they could base the ministry of their dreams.

The main house was enough to get started. Then, over time, John converted their huge Amish-style barn into six cozy, well-appointed rooms. It was slow going at first. Who really wants to spend vacation time learning how to better communicate and plan? But as couples began experiencing what the Finches offered, word spread. Through strong testimonies and a robust social network, couples from all over the northeast began staying at Village Crest.

Rob and Sarah Mills represent a "typical" couple going to the Village Crest Inn. They left their children with the grandparents and looked forward to a weekend of planning for their future.

"There it is, Rob!" Sarah shouted as she pointed across the roadway.

"Where?" Rob asked as he continued to negotiate the sharp S-turns.

"Well, it's back there now!" said Sarah, looking back. "You just passed it."

"No way!" Rob replied. "Nobody puts a sign right in a curve."

"I guess you're right. That probably wasn't it after all. But it sure looked like a B&B sign," Sarah insisted.

"Really, Sarah? What do B&B signs look like anyway?" Rob asked.

"Well, you know. They're not metal. They're more homespun-type signs."

"Homespun-type signs? Oh yeah, that's good," Rob said. "You come up with some of the most ridiculous categories for things. Do you know that?"

"*Creative* categories!" corrected Sarah. "You just fail to see it, that's all."

"Whatever!" Rob said. "Just pull out those 10 tourist maps you stuck in the glove box and see if one of them has this place on it. If we don't find the inn by dark, we'll be in a world of hurt in these mountains."

"Isn't this amazing, Rob?" Sarah asked as she looked at the trees through the sunroof. "I think we hit the fall colors right at their peak."

"Fascinating!" Rob responded. "Now, will you *please* get the map out and see how far we have to go?"

Sarah fumbled through the glove box and extracted a map. She awkwardly unfolded it and studied it for a few minutes. "Oh my word!" she exclaimed.

"'Oh my word' what?" Rob said. "Don't tell me we're on the wrong road!"

"No, we're fine," Sarah said. "But do you have any idea what's right ahead?"

"Our destination maybe?"

"Better than that! The Blow-Me-Down Covered Bridge. It's just up ahead. We need to take some pictures of that!"

"Sarah, we've stopped at what, seven bridges so far today? I'm not stopping at another one! I'm over the covered bridge thing," Rob said. "Besides, they all look alike."

"Well, of course they look alike to you!" Sarah replied. "You have to actually *look* at the bridges to see the differences in them."

"Well, there it is," Rob pointed out. "Snap a picture as we go by!"

"You know everything doesn't have to be an aerobic exercise, Rob," Sarah said. "Relax."

"Hey! I agreed to come on this retreat, didn't I? I'm missing a huge meeting at work," Rob snapped.

"Yeah…and it only took two years to get you to agree," Sarah responded.

"Taking time off is pretty hard when I have five mouths to feed," Rob said. "It's all I can do just to make enough to keep us afloat."

As they passed through Blow-Me-Down Covered Bridge, Sarah felt her heart sinking fast. She wanted a picture in front of each bridge they crossed. Her parents often did that on their trips. They loved to take time for the little things, and Sarah was raised to do the same. But Rob was the polar opposite. He lived in a hurried, bottom-line-is-everything, no-time-to-communicate world. Why he agreed to this planning retreat was beyond Sarah's comprehension. If Rob had his way, she was sure their weekend retreat would be over in two hours max.

When they finally pulled into the Village Crest Inn parking lot, Rob breathed a sigh of relief. "Finally! I thought we'd never get here."

As they entered the office, the woman behind the counter greeted them with a smile. "Welcome to Village Crest! We're so glad to have you here. You must be Sarah and Rob. My name's Dottie. Let's get you checked in. Did you have any trouble finding us?"

"Yes, we're Rob and Sarah. And it sure wasn't easy getting here," Rob answered. "There are so many sharp turns it's easy to not notice the driveways until you're almost past them."

"That's true, Rob," Dottie agreed as she pulled up their reservation. "John says that road is a lot like people."

"Oh? In what way?" Rob asked.

"Both are full of blind spots," Dottie said with a smile as she continued checking the couple in. "Ah, you're in the C.S. Lewis room, which is the first room on the left as you enter the Amish barn. You can park right in front. Dinner is at seven. Do you need any help with your bags?"

"No, we'll be fine," Rob said. After registering, the couple returned to their car.

Rob pulled the car in front of the barn and unloaded the luggage. Inside, the room was small but tastefully done with an unmistakable focal point. Two wingback chairs by the window facing one another. Sarah eyed the packet on the table between the two chairs. When she saw their names on it, she knew this B&B was just as advertised—a place with purpose.

"What's that?" Rob asked as he walked in with the last suitcase.

"It looks like a packet to get our weekend started," Sarah replied. "It has our names on it."

"I'd rather it be mints and stuff!" Rob joked as he opened the envelope. He read aloud:

Dear Rob and Sarah,

Welcome to Village Crest Inn! We are John and Dottie, your hosts. We've been married for 31 years. For the first 15 years, we totally missed out on the happiness we should have had. We were so confident in our own abilities that we put very little stock in each other's gifts. We were so concerned about what we wanted that we had no concern for what the other person needed. It wasn't a pretty picture. We made and spent our own money. We did what we wanted when we wanted. We just happened to land in the same bed at the end of the day.

We were amiable, efficient, happy-go-lucky, money-making machines. But on the inside, we were void of real life and as empty as two human beings could possibly be. But then something happened that changed all that. Now we have more than we ever dreamed possible!

When we committed our lives to Jesus Christ and He came into our lives, He brought some profound changes. Next to our salvation, the biggest impact was in our marriage. God radically altered the way we viewed each other. We quit *looking* for the person we wanted to be with and began *becoming* the person the other one was looking for.

Since then, our goal has been to help other couples find the happiness we've found. Our prayer for you during your time with us is that you'll rediscover the person God created especially for you. We're here to help any way we can.

Sincerely,
John and Dottie

"That might be the sweetest thing I've ever heard!" Sarah said, dabbing at a tear.

"I don't know about sweet, but it sure is nervy," Rob said. "I came here to get away and plan for next year. I didn't come here to get lectured. And did you notice the rest of this stuff? There are two questions and then eight decisions we're supposed to talk about. I'm not sure I'm up for this."

"What are the questions?" Sarah asked.

"The first one is 'Do you and your spouse enjoy talking to one another?' What kind of question is that?"

"Well, how would you answer it?" Sarah asked.

"What do you mean? I love talking to you," Rob answered.

"You mean as long as it doesn't take more than five minutes!" Sarah shot back.

"So I won't sit around and talk for hours on end like you and your sister do. I admit that," Rob conceded. "But that doesn't mean I don't enjoy talking to you."

"You enjoy talking when it's on *your* terms," Sarah answered quickly. "Keep going. What's the second question?"

Rob looked at the paper. "Is there any topic you and your spouse avoid talking about?"

"Well?" Sarah asked.

"Absolutely not! You can't name one thing I avoid talking about!"

"Well, we certainly don't talk about money," Sarah corrected.

"Yes, we do," Rob said. "We talk about money all the time."

"We talk about what *you've decided* about our money," Sarah corrected again. "Or you pretend to get my input, but then you don't really consider it. That's very different than actually discussing it."

"Well, that's my job," Rob responded. "I make the money and keep the books. I don't *avoid* talking about money. I just don't need to talk to you about it because I understand money better than you do."

We'll return to Rob and Sarah's planning weekend shortly, but first I want to note that their story weaves throughout this book to point out far-too-common scenarios I've witnessed as I've consulted with couples in my practice as a financial adviser. Although money provides tremendous freedom and can be used to do great and noble things for the kingdom of God, in many marriages money is a source of friction, frustration, and anxiety. Research shows that

> conflict over money matters is one of the most important problems in contemporary married life. Compared with disagreements over other topics, financial disagreements last longer, are more salient to couples, and generate more negative conflict tactics, such as yelling or hitting, especially among husbands. Perhaps because they are socialized to be providers, men seem to take financial conflict particularly hard. Not surprisingly, new research...indicates conflict over money matters predicts divorce better than other types of disagreement.[1]

Clearly Sarah and Rob have challenges when it comes to money, and their communication issues go even deeper. They love each other, but they don't understand the way God created and "wired" them uniquely. The same is true for most of us who are married. We would do well to be good students of our spouses—seeking by God's grace to understand, respect, love, and encourage one another in all areas.

The purpose of this book is to address the specific challenges couples face regarding money. I'll use Rob and Sarah to illustrate the typical financial conflicts that arise between couples.

First, why do Sarah and Rob have so much trouble communicating about money? Why don't they seem to see eye to eye? To answer that, let's back up and ask a more basic question: Why is money such a source of conflict?

Reasons for Conflicts About Money

My observation is that there are three underlying reasons money causes so many marital problems:

- incorrect thinking
- lack of communication
- not having a game plan

Let's take a closer look at each of these.

Incorrect Thinking

Many couples simply don't think correctly about money or about marriage. Our culture has so influenced our thinking in these two areas that we've come to believe what the world says to be true rather than what God says to be true. Let me illustrate.

- *The world says money is the key to happiness.* When we believe this as truth, we place a high value on making money. This consumes the better part of our day and the majority of our thinking. Money, however, *isn't* the key to happiness. In the most affluent countries in the world, we see individuals and families who have all the material trappings they could ever desire and yet they are not happy. The *real* truth is that we're truly happy only when we are rightly connected to God through Jesus Christ (John 10:10).

- *The world says that the accumulation of money will meet our needs and give us worth, acceptance, and significance.* This "fact" is evidenced by our pursuit of money and our lack of devotion to our marriages, our children, and God. Too often we sacrifice our relationships on the altar of money. The *real* truth is that our worth is a function of who we are in Christ and not what we own materially (Luke 12:16-21). The truth is that our legacy (and what will last) is people (Psalm 37:37-38; Ecclesiastes 5:15). The truth is that we are more fulfilled and content when we enjoy a harmonious and loving marriage relationship with our spouse (Ecclesiastes 9:9).

- *The world says that the ultimate goal in life is to achieve ease, comfort, and pleasure, and accumulating money is the ticket to get there.* I believe this worldly truth is evidenced by how we set our priorities and our insatiable desire to get ahead at all costs. We put a premium on being able to "arrive" by using words and phrases such as "retire," "make it," "strike it rich," and "go for the gold." The *real* truth, however, is that the more a person has, the more he or she wants. The Bible rightly tells us, "He who loves money will not be satisfied with money" (Ecclesiastes 5:10). The *real* ultimate goal in life is to learn to be content and enjoy life without seeking "to arrive" (Philippians 4:11). The *real* truth is that we will encounter trials (1 Thessalonians 3:2-3). Ease, comfort, and pleasure in this life are not promised by God.

- *The world says that the purpose of our marriage relationship is to meet our needs and make us happy.* We believe our spouses are with us to meet our needs and assist us in our never-ending pursuit of ease, comfort, and pleasure. This is evidenced by the rampant divorce rate in this country. Once our needs cease to be met the way we think they should be, we try another spouse. The *real* truth is that our marriage relationship was ordained by God for *His* glory and our fulfillment (Genesis 2:18). Marriage relationships were intended by God to be for life. He hates divorce (Malachi 2:16).

Incorrect thinking has caused many couples to lose perspective and, as a consequence, put their marriages at risk. A good perspective involves keeping things in proper relationship to one another and thinking correctly. In this case, the key is keeping money and our marriages in proper relation to each other and thinking about them the way God does.

Lack of Communication

The second basic problem is lack of communication. Good communication occurs when each spouse has listened and fully comprehended what the other has said and understands how the other feels and why the person feels as he or she does.

Many couples seem to have a difficult time communicating, especially in the area of money. In most cases, we don't understand what our spouses are saying, let alone know why they feel the way they do. Rob and Sarah were able to talk *about* money, but no real communication was taking place. They hadn't taken the time to really understand each other.

Julie, my wife, and I found that it was difficult to set aside time to communicate, especially when it involved money. Much time is needed to discuss a budget, develop a workable cash-control system, and talk about investments, insurance, and wills. Although it does take significant effort, Julie and I determined that our marriage was important enough to *make* the time. Hopefully as you read this book you will come to the same conclusion.

No Game Plan

The last problem is having no predetermined goals or plans regarding finances. No one would start out on a vacation without a destination and a plan as to how he was going to get there. Yet, many of us start our marriages without plans for handling money.

It's vital that we married couples develop a plan so we will avoid many of the tensions that arise when we get in the middle of a financial situation. As couples, we need to agree *beforehand* on how we will handle money, deal with financial conflicts, and make monetary decisions. A plan will enable us to turn a possible conflict into a positive experience rather than a potential marriage breaker.

I can't state strongly enough the need for good premarital counseling. Going into marriage with a good understanding of how you both will handle finances (as well as many other areas of life) will be a boon to your marriage. Consider pastoral counseling or, at a minimum, find a good resource to go through together. Many are available, including Les and Leslie Parrott's *Saving Your Marriage Before It Starts*.

How This Book Can Help You

My purpose in writing this book is to provide insights that will help you overcome potential marriage conflicts that often occur as a result of money problems. In chapters 1 through 4, we'll look at the biblical purposes of money and work, reasons for marriage, and typical reasons for financial conflicts. In chapters 5 through 12, we'll examine eight specific financial decisions that each couple must wrestle through to establish a solid financial plan. This includes how much we should work, bill paying, living expenses, budgeting, debt load, investments, and giving.

We'll also look at why communication is so difficult when it comes to these topics. Every chapter will conclude with questions to help facilitate discussion and growth between your spouse and you.

The final chapter is special in that it is written by my wife, Julie. George Fooshee, author of *Your Money: A Biblical Guide to Personal Money Management* and *You Can Beat the Money Squeeze*, after reading the original manuscript, said, "It is the finest treatment on the woman's role in finances I have seen and is a must-read for wives and husbands."

It's my sincere hope that as you read this book you'll gain a fresh perspective on money and your marriage. With this more comprehensive view, I trust you'll have a better appreciation of why money has so much potential for destroying marital harmony and unity. I pray you will conclude, as Julie and I have, that marriage is special and worth any effort required to keep it strong, vibrant, and supportive. We've found the following two portions of Scripture to be great sources of motivation in putting forth the necessary effort to achieve a successful, fulfilling marriage:

> To sum up, all of you be harmonious, sympathetic, brotherly, kind-hearted, and humble in spirit; not returning evil for evil or insult for insult, but giving a blessing instead; for you were called for the very purpose that you might inherit a blessing (1 Peter 3:8-9).
>
> Make my joy complete by being of the same mind, maintaining the same love, united in spirit, intent on one purpose (Philippians 2:2).

May God richly bless your marriage!

Part 1

The Foundation

Chapter 1

The Purpose of Money

Money. Not a day goes by that most of us don't think about it, work for it, or spend it. Money is, in fact, necessary for our well-being and our ability to function in society. However, without a proper understanding of money it can consume us. So what is the truth about money? Why do we have to have it? How do we get it? Is it really worth all the time and effort we invest in trying to make it? How should we spend it when we do get it? Does having a lot of it make us important and successful?

After 30 years of counseling hundreds of couples about their finances, I'm convinced that if people can come to grips with the real purpose of money and understand the truth about it from God's perspective, their lives and marriages will benefit greatly. Let's look, then, at the purpose of money, beginning with what it is not.

What Money Is Not

When I was a boy, I was involved in a small business. As a part of a 4-H Club project, I had a flock of sheep. By buying and selling lambs, including showing them at the county fair as an opportunity to make sales, I was able to generate a profit and have money in my pocket at the end of fair week. I well remember walking around the fairgrounds with feelings of confidence and positive self-worth as a result of the money in my pocket. I felt good about myself.

One time I spent quite a bit of money at the fair. My feelings of confidence and self-worth were damaged as the cash dwindled away. I felt worse about myself. But was I really any different than when I had the money?

As I reflect on that time in my youth, I realize that I had already bought the world's lie that my worth as a person had something to do with the amount of money I had. Like so many people, I didn't know the truth about money. So let's look, then, at the truth about money as revealed in the Bible.

Money Is Not a Component of Self-Worth

The first thing we must understand is that money *is not* a necessary component of our self-worth. If I don't accept this truth, if I believe that my self-worth is related to the money I have, then my self-worth will vacillate depending on my income and net worth at any given time. I will tend to feel that I'm of value only if I make a certain amount of income. Such false thinking is totally contrary to what the Scripture says about who we are in Christ and the ultimate source of our income.

We don't need to look very far in the Bible to see how valuable we are in God's view. In the very first chapter we see God, the Creator of the universe, considering man of such value and worth that He chose to create him in His own image and according to His likeness (Genesis 1:26-27). And in Psalm 8:3-6 we read:

> When I consider Your heavens, the work of Your fingers,
> The moon and the stars, which You have ordained;
> What is man that You take thought of him,
> And the son of man that You care for him?
> Yet You have made him a little lower than God,
> And You crown him with glory and majesty!
> You make him to rule over the works of Your hands;
> You have put all things under his feet.

In the New Testament, we see again that we are God's workmanship, hand-fashioned by Him (Ephesians 2:10). We also see the ultimate expression of our worth to Him in John 3:16: "God so loved the world, that He gave His only begotten Son, that whoever believes in Him shall not perish, but have eternal life."

That means we're each worth an incredible amount to God. Yet we typically evaluate a person's worth by how much money that person accumulates or earns. Money is all too often a concrete standard of merit used in rating ourselves.

> *If we want healthy marriages, we must learn to detach our self-worth from our money.*

Bill Gillham, in his book *Lifetime Guarantee,* made a list of scriptural truths about you and me as Christians. These include the facts that we are seated with Christ in the heavenlies, we are joint heirs with Christ, we are near to God, we are new creatures in Christ, we are liberated, and we are complete in Him.[1]

Clearly, from God's point of view our value has nothing to do with our net worth or the income we earn. Our merit has *everything* to do with who we are in Christ and what God says about us. You and I have a choice. We can believe what God says or we can believe what the world says. God says that we are valuable whether we have much or little money.

If we want healthy marriages, we must learn to detach our self-worth from our money. This is especially true for husbands. Scripture tells us that we men need to love our wives as our own bodies (Ephesians 5:28). And if I'm going to love the way God intends, I need to embrace my worth as a beloved child of God. If I allow money to be a factor in my self-image, I run the risk of having my love and devotion to my spouse vacillate with my income. I can't afford to take that risk if I want harmony in my marriage. Neither can you.

Money Is Not a Guarantee of Contentment

Money can't guarantee contentment. Contentment can be defined as "being satisfied with one's circumstances; not complaining; not craving something else; and having a mind at peace." I'm convinced that true contentment has nothing to do with money. A person may have a lot of money or a little bit of money and *still* miss the whole point of contentment. He can complain whether he has a little or a lot. He can be covetous just as easily with a lot of money as with a little. Solomon wrote, "He who loves money will not be satisfied with money, nor he who loves abundance with its income. This too is vanity" (Ecclesiastes 5:10).

> *Only as I realize that God is sovereign and providentially in control of my earthly lot can I truly be content.*

Contentment is a learned response. Paul stated this very clearly: "Not that I speak from want, for I have *learned* to be content in whatever circumstances I am. I know how to get along with humble means, and I also know how to live in prosperity; in any and every circumstance I have learned the secret of being filled and going hungry, both of having abundance and suffering need" (Philippians 4:11-12).

The secret Paul was alluding to was a result of learning to think rightly about money and God. Part of contentment is learning to see money as God sees it. It's also learning to see God for who He is. He is the bedrock of our contentment. I like what Major W. Ian Thomas says in his book *The Saving Life of Christ:* "All you need is what you have; what you have is what He is; you cannot have more; and you do not need to have less."[2]

Only as I realize that God is sovereign and providentially in control of my earthly lot (my vocation and income) can I truly be content. Only as I learn to trust Him can I have true contentment. Only as I realize that the creator God of the universe loves me and has my best interests at heart can I be fully content. Contentment really is a spiritual issue, not an amount-of-money issue. God is always with us, and He never changes. He is consistent and stable. We can trust Him.

What about money? Proverbs 23:4-5 speaks to this: "Do not weary yourself to gain wealth, cease from your consideration of it. When you set your eyes on it, it is gone. For wealth certainly makes itself wings, like an eagle that flies toward the heavens." How content can we be in something that flies away?

No principle in this book will have a greater impact on you and free you more than this essential truth: *Money is not the key to contentment!*

Contentment has everything to do with your relationship with God and nothing to do with money. Once you are free from the love of money and the pursuit of it, you can have a lot or a little and be content all the same.

Before leaving this discussion of contentment, let me add a definition of *financial* contentment. "Financial contentment" is simply "living within one's income." How we handle what God has given us will result in whether we achieve financial contentment. I remember a trip where I'd met with a man who earned in excess of $600,000 a year. Instead of being content and at peace, he was miserable. He had financial pressure because he was spending $100,000 more than he was making. I commented to my wife that the key to contentment in one's finances is not the amount one makes but rather a willingness to live within that amount.

Are you thinking, "Russ, if I made $600,000 I would be content"? But the truth is, *if you are not content in your current financial position, you would not be content if you had more money.* Julie and I have found that our marriage is peaceful when, first of all, we are committed to live within our income—whatever it is—and, second, when we refuse to focus on and put our confidence in the income we do have.

Money Is Not a Measure of Success

To illustrate the truth that money doesn't measure success, consider a doctor and a teacher. Each can do an excellent job and be successful at his or her vocational calling, and yet the income each generates probably varies greatly. The doctor may earn 10 times what the teacher earns and spend less time doing it. In this case, money obviously isn't a good measure of success. It's even more obvious when you consider that a doctor could do a mediocre job and still earn more than a teacher who does an excellent job.

God has equipped and called each of us to uniquely fill the myriad jobs He needs done to fulfill His purposes. Therefore, God—who sovereignly ordains my job—ultimately determines my income. My income isn't so much a function of my success or failure as it is just one part of my God-appointed vocation.

I don't want to discount that an excellent job on your part may cause you to earn more than someone else who doesn't work as excellently or diligently in the same vocation. My caution to you is to be careful not to believe *your ability* is generating your income. Deuteronomy 8:16-18 is clear on this point: "Otherwise, you may say in your heart, 'My power and the strength of my hand made me this wealth.' But you shall remember the LORD your God, for it is He who is giving you power to make wealth." If you're having difficulty accepting the idea that God is providentially in control of your income, consider these Scriptures:

- The rich and the poor have a common bond, the LORD is the maker of them all (Proverbs 22:2).
- What do you have that you did not receive? (1 Corinthians 4:7).
- Every good thing given and every perfect gift is from above (James 1:17).

Remember too that life is full of financial inequities, just as Solomon reminds us: "I again saw under the sun that the race is not to the swift and the battle is not to the warriors, and neither is bread to the wise nor wealth to the discerning nor favor to men of ability; for time and chance overtake them all" (Ecclesiastes 9:11).

The world tells us one sign of success is how much money we make. However, if we look up the definition of "success," we see that we're successful *if we are making progress in accomplishing our goals.* Success occurs when we satisfactorily complete what we attempt. Money may be one result of our endeavors, but it should never be the standard in determining whether success has occurred. Interestingly, the words "prosperity" and "prosperous" have basically the same meaning as success.

I had a problem totally understanding Joshua 1:8 until I applied the correct definition of success and prosperity. Joshua 1:8 says:

This book of the law shall not depart from your mouth, but you shall meditate on it day and night, so that you may be careful to do according to all that is written in it; for then you will make your way prosperous, and then you will have success.

I'm only successful and prosperous to the extent that I'm being obedient and carefully doing all that God's Word says to do. For example, I'm successful as I train and love my children (Ephesians 6:4; Deuteronomy 6:6-7), love my wife (Ephesians 5:28), and work hard (Colossians 3:23). Joshua 1:8 doesn't guarantee or promise financial blessings if I do what God's Word says. Rather, it frees me to realize that I can be successful and prosperous *whether or not I have money*. Money is not the barometer! A successful person may or may not have money. A person with money may or may not be a success.

> *Much of the stress in our marriages is a result of using money as a measuring stick to determine our level of success.*

Years ago, a friend of mine began developing and growing a very profitable business. It soon went public, and my friend was acclaimed a success by his industry and the media. Everybody wanted a piece of the action. His net worth was in the millions, and in the world's eyes he was a success. As the years wore on, however, this man's business declined. Although my friend did all he could to keep the business afloat, it eventually went bankrupt. My friend's net worth plummeted. Was my friend still a success? Many would probably say no because the world's measuring stick is money, and he no longer had financial wealth. However, I know better. During that time frame, my friend made more progress in the things that are important to God than most people knew. His relationship with his family and the Lord improved dramatically. He had significant impact on other people's lives. He was still a success when his money was gone because he had made progress in accomplishing many of the goals God says are important.

Much of the stress in our marriages is a result of using money as a measuring stick to determine our level of success. We need to change our standard of measuring success from money to what God's Word says.

What Money Is

According to the dictionary, "money" is "a medium of exchange;

any equivalent for commodities; something for which individuals readily exchange their goods or services; a circulating medium." As such, money must satisfy three basic functions. It must be storable, divisible, and valuable. Money today still has the first two components, but in a practical sense it no longer has any real value. For instance, up until 1933, the United States held to a gold standard that required all paper money issued be backed by a fixed quantity of gold. At any time a person could exchange their paper money for gold. At that time the real money was gold, which has value, but paper was used as a substitute since it was more easily divisible and easier to store than the gold it represented.

The reason the United States government eventually departed from the gold standard was to allow itself and banks to inflate or deflate the money supply to smooth out the normal business cycles of inflations and retractions (booms and busts). They thought that if they could smooth out the cycles by issuing more or less credit, depending on what the economy "needed" at the time, there would be more consistent prosperity for all. At the time of writing this book, the issue of currency (money) debasement is a hot topic. The "medium of exchange" in many countries, including the United States, is under attack.

Although money is potentially becoming worth less, the items we purchase with it have utilitarian value. The clothes we wear, our homes, our investments in real property, and even our investments in credit instruments such as bonds and CDs all have some form of value because they are useful to us. They help us exist, provide for our families, and meet our needs.

To show just how overrated money is and how our perspective of it has totally gotten out of whack, let's look for a minute at 2 Corinthians 4:18: "We look not at the things which are seen, but at the things which are not seen; for the things which are seen are temporal, but the things which are not seen are eternal." Money is a medium of exchange that we can see and touch. It is purely temporal and thus not something on which God says we should focus.

What happens to all the things we can buy with money? First Timothy 6:7 says, "We have brought nothing into the world, so we cannot take anything out of it either." In Ecclesiastes 5:15, we read that nothing from the fruit of our labor (purchased with our money) can be taken with us. Psalm 49:17 continues this theme when it says, "When he dies he will carry nothing away."

Wow! God's Word indicates that money is not eternal, and we can take none of it with us when we die. Money is simply a medium of exchange useful during this lifetime but of no eternal significance. Recently I saw a church billboard that said, "Your children are your only earthly possession that can go to heaven." How insightful! That thought should help us keep money in correct perspective.

If in a practical sense money is a merely a mode of exchange, what is it from God's perspective? How does He view it? In *Master Your Money*, author Ron Blue uses three words to summarize how God views money: tool, test, and testimony.

Money as a Tool

God uses countless tools to mold us into His image, and money is one of them. Just as the craftsman uses the tools of his trade to form a final product that's pleasing to him, so God uses money (its abundance and its scarcity) to mold us and make us pleasing to Him. He did that with the apostle Paul. As I noted before, Paul was taught contentment by the extremes of having much (abundance) and little (scarcity) (Philippians 4:11-12).

You may have thought God only uses the *lack* of money to mold and train and form a person into His image. I can assure you that is not the case. In my financial consulting, I've observed that the person with wealth has to learn how to deal with greed, how to share, how to exhibit wise stewardship, how to love and maintain relationships, how to use time wisely, and how to deal with the fear of losing money. Money's use as a tool is effective at *all* levels of income.

Money as a Test

Money is also used as a test in our lives. It's a test of our faithfulness to God. Luke 16:11-13 reads:

> If you have not been faithful in the use of unrighteous wealth, who will entrust the true riches to you? And if you have not been faithful in the use of that which is another's, who will give you that which is your own?

> No servant can serve two masters; for either he will hate the one and love the other, or else he will be devoted to one and despise the other. You cannot serve God and wealth.

You notice that the verse doesn't say that we "should not" serve both or that we should "try not to" serve both. It says we *cannot* serve both! Either I will serve God and use money to serve people, or I will use people to serve myself and use money for myself. As Philip Yancey wrote: "Money is far more than a question of statistics and numbers, it is a god that bids us worship it. Will I serve God or mammon? God will never make that decision for me; it is mine alone."[3] Randy Alcorn, in *Money, Possessions, & Eternity,* warns of the spiritual dangers of loving money:

> Idolatry is worshipping and serving anything other than the one true God. Everything we have, including money, is either a tool or an idol. If we fail to use it as a tool for God's intended purposes, it mutates into an idol. For the Church, the bride of Christ, idolatry is the same as adultery—a wanton betrayal of a husband who loves us enough to die for us.[4]

We need to regularly ask ourselves diagnostic questions and ask God to show us the state of our hearts. Are we, as individuals, as couples, and as families, serving God? Or are we becoming enamored with the ways of the world? Do our schedules reflect our commitment to God's kingdom? Do our patterns of giving to the church and other ministries reflect that we value what God values?

Money as a Testimony

Finally, money is a testimony. We read this in Matthew 5:13-16:

> You are the salt of the earth; but if the salt has become tasteless, how can it be made salty again? It is no longer good for anything, except to be thrown out and trampled under foot by men. You are the light of the world. A city set on a hill cannot be hidden; nor does anyone light a lamp and put it under a basket, but on the lampstand, and it gives light to all who are in the house. Let your light shine before men in such a way that they may see your good works, and glorify your Father who is in heaven.

What kind of a testimony do I give with my money? Does it bring glory and honor to God? As Christians, we're not called to be *better* than the world when it comes to our money; rather, we are called to be *different* from the world. Each of us needs to look at our finances and ask: What kind of a statement am I making to the world with the way I handle my money? Could anyone tell by looking at my checkbook that I'm a Christian?

When we talk about being different and being generous to those around us, what does that mean? For Julie and me, it has meant driving the cars a little longer, living in a smaller house a few more years, and making sure we're living within our income year in and year out. And lest we think folks aren't watching, I was reminded they are when a woman shared this with me:

> I heard you speak, but I wasn't sure I wanted to believe you. Then I saw you and your wife shopping one evening at the grocery store, so I followed you around. I wanted to see what you bought. And then I followed you into the parking lot to see what you were driving. You really did practice what you preached (coupons at the store and driving an older car), so I decided I could trust you.

Needless to say, it's a little spooky to consider being watched at the grocery store, but the fact is, we are each testifying to something with our lives. This lady was checking out whether or not Julie and I were really living differently than most of the world. I don't know what "different" might look like for you, but my experience is that the closer I order my life in obedience to God in this money area, the more likely my life will look different.

Conclusion

If we don't know the truth about money (its purpose), our focus on it can be so intense that it can ruin marriages. This is why money is so dangerous. Having a proper, biblical view of money will go a long way in helping us prioritize our marriage relationships over money. So remember:

- Money is not a component of self-worth.
- Money is not a guarantee of contentment.
- Money is not a measure of success.
- Money is often a medium God uses in our lives as a tool, a test, and a testimony.

Game Plan

1. What do you think about the definitions of "success" presented?

2. Why is incorrect thinking about money so prevalent today?

3. How has money been a test for you?

4. What kind of testimony would your checkbook reveal?

5. Are you content with what you have? Why or why not?

Chapter 2

The Purpose of Marriage

Having looked at the purpose of money, we now turn to a second vital issue: the purpose of marriage. So why do we marry? God ordained marriage primarily to show His glory, but marriage is also a gift to us! It is a holy union that should bring us the highest level of earthly enjoyment and blessing. While that's often true, if we're forthright we must admit that good marriages are a lot of work. Mike Mason, in his book *The Mystery of Marriage*, writes honestly when he says:

> Marriage has been devised by the Lord as a particularly gentle (but no less disciplined and effective) means for helping men and women to humble themselves and to surrender their errant wills. Even the closest of couples will inevitably find themselves engaged in a struggle of wills, for marriage is a wild, audacious attempt at an almost impossible degree of cooperation between two powerful centers of self-assertion. Marriage cannot help being a furnace of conflict, a crucible in which two wills must be melted down and purified and made to conform.[1]

Marriage has many aims; however, four relate to our financial discussion:

- Marriage allows us to model Christ and the church.
- Marriage allows us to model biblical male/female roles.

- Marriage allows us to procreate.
- Marriage allows us an opportunity to raise godly posterity—children who will have a positive impact on the generations to come.

To Model Christ and the Church

In this passage from the book of Ephesians, we see the clear calling that marriage is to be a model of Christ and the church:

> Wives, be subject to your own husbands, as to the Lord. For the husband is the head of the wife, as Christ also is the head of the church, He Himself being the Savior of the body. But as the church is subject to Christ, so also the wives ought to be to their husbands in everything. Husbands, love your wives, just as Christ also loved the church and gave Himself up for her, so that He might sanctify her, having cleansed her by the washing of water with the word, that He might present to Himself the church in all her glory, having no spot or wrinkle or any such thing; but that she would be holy and blameless. So husbands ought also to love their own wives as their own bodies. He who loves his own wife loves himself; for no one ever hated his own flesh, but nourishes and cherishes it, just as Christ also does the church, because we are members of His body. For this reason a man shall leave his father and mother and shall be joined to his wife, and the two shall become one flesh. This mystery is great; but I am speaking with reference to Christ and the church. Nevertheless, each individual among you also is to love his own wife even as himself, and the wife must see to it that she respects her husband (5:22-33).

As the adage says, "The only Bible some people will ever read is our lives." If people are reading our marriages, what do they see? Do they want to have a relationship with God because our marriages are so attractive and work so well they can't resist? Or does what they see cause them to want to have nothing to do with God? As Christians, we're called to bring glory to Christ. One of the chief ways we can do that is by having harmonious, God-honoring, loving marriages.

Let's look at the Ephesians 5:23-33 passage and reflect on the primary responsibilities of husbands to love their wives and wives to submit to and respect their husbands if our marriages are to model Christ and the church. This, by the way, doesn't mean that the wife is not to love her husband or that the husband is not to submit to or respect his wife. The responsibilities listed in this Ephesians passage are not mutually exclusive. For our discussion, however, we'll focus on these responsibilities as being unique to each spouse.

Husband, Love Your Wife

Husbands, we are instructed to love our wives as Christ loved the church and as we love our own bodies. The quality of our marriages depends on our ability to love our wives to the fullest definition of the word. Using 1 Corinthians 13:4-8 as our guide, let's look at how the qualities of this love will manifest themselves to our wives in the realm of finances.

> Love is patient, love is kind and is not jealous; love does not brag and is not arrogant, does not act unbecomingly; it does not seek its own, is not provoked, does not take into account a wrong suffered, does not rejoice in unrighteousness, but rejoices with the truth; bears all things, believes all things, hopes all things, endures all things.

1. *Love is patient.* The husband tolerates problems that arise and is patient with his wife regardless of her behavior. He endures offense from his wife even when he feels like retaliating. He responds with patience when she doesn't handle circumstances exactly the way he wants her to. (For example, he takes time to discuss an investment with her and doesn't become exasperated when she doesn't agree with his decision.)

2. *Love is kind.* The husband is good-natured, thoughtful, gentle, and sensitive to his wife. (He gets her input on financial matters.)

3. *Love is never jealous or envious.* The husband trusts his wife completely and thinks only the best of her. He always assumes her motives and intentions are right. (He lets his wife know that he trusts her to spend "their" money by giving her maximum freedom in the financial budget.)

4. *Love is never rude.* The husband is not unmannerly and is careful to avoid embarrassing his wife. (He does not speak down to her if she doesn't understand finances as well as he does.)

5. *Love is unselfish.* The husband doesn't seek his own convenience and rights but rather looks out for his wife's best interests and is concerned about her. (He seeks to meet her needs financially.)

6. *Love is not irritable or touchy.* The husband keeps his temper and exhibits self-control. (When she spends money in a way he doesn't understand, he talks it over with her in a controlled, calm manner.)

7. *Love never holds a grudge.* The husband doesn't keep score and return evil for evil (1 Peter 3:9). He forgives and forgets. (If his wife overspends one month, he doesn't overreact or withhold money from her the next month.)

8. *Love rejoices in right.* The husband exults in his wife's successes and is never glad about her misfortunes. (He compliments her for the way she handles the budget and for her wise spending habits.)

9. *Love is loyal and dependable.* The husband is faithful to his wife. She knows she can always count on him. He is never "on and off"; instead, he is stable and consistent. (He communicates with her at all times, not just when he wants something. He doesn't vary the monthly budget amounts without seeking her input and understanding.)

I don't know about you, but following the biblical pattern of love is daunting! Only by yielding to Christ and walking by the power of the Holy Spirit will we be able to love our wives with the *agape* (self-sacrificing) love God requires. You may be thinking you're incapable of showing love in the ways we just discussed. You may feel it's too much trouble to communicate about the budget or investments or to give your wife maximum freedom with the finances. If that's the way you feel now, this book is for you. Please keep reading.

Wife, Submit to and Respect Your Husband

Wives, your part in ensuring your marriages model Christ and the church is to respect your husband and to submit to him. I know these words aren't especially popular today. Many would have us believe that submission means inferiority. Yet this is not what God's Word intends. Bryan Chapell says in *Each for the Other,* "Wives [should submit] not as meek and mindless mice, but by making full use of their gifts for the support of the husbands God commits to their care."[2]

So how do we think biblically about submission? True "submission" is simply understanding God's order and fitting into that order. Submission is yielding to God's design for marriage (see chart 2.1 on next page). Notably, husbands have responsibility both ways. Not only are they to love their wives, but they are also told to submit and understand their wives (1 Peter 3:7). A spirit of graceful submission is required on the part of each spouse, and there can be no peace or harmony without it. And the response of one spouse is not dependent on the other. No matter how our spouses respond, we are responsible to respond the way God instructs. "So then each one of us will give an account of himself to God" (Romans 14:12).

Mutual submission can be illustrated in the living expenses area of a family's finances. The wife should submit and live within the amount agreed upon for living expenses. The husband should listen to and give deference to his wife's desires regarding the appropriate amounts in the various categories. For example, who usually has a better understanding of how much to budget for kids' clothes and groceries, the husband or wife? The critical ingredient on the part of the wife is her attitude. Submission is an attitude and view of life that is consistent with God's view:

> In the same way, you wives, be submissive to your own husbands so that even if any of them are disobedient to the word, they may be won without a word by the behavior of their wives (1 Peter 3:1).
>
> [Older women are to encourage younger women] to be self-controlled, chaste, homemakers, good-natured (kindhearted), adapting and subordinating themselves to their husbands, that the word of God may not be exposed to reproach (blasphemed or discredited) (Titus 2:5 AMP).

Respect is the other responsibility of the wife in the marriage relationship. What that word entails is best summed up in 1 Peter 3:2:

> …when they observe the pure and modest way in which you conduct yourselves, together with your reverence [for your husband; you are to feel for him all that reverence includes: to respect, defer to, revere him—to honor, esteem, appreciate, prize, and, in the human sense, adore him, that is, to admire, praise, be devoted to, deeply love, and enjoy your husband] (AMP, brackets in original).

Financially, this means a wife defers to her husband, honors him, and respects his wishes and decisions concerning how she spends money. She makes sure that she always asks or thinks, "What have we agreed to do with our money?"

If our marriages are to model Christ and the church, then husbands must love their wives with self-sacrificing, *agape* love and wives must respect and submit to their husbands. If husbands and wives will focus on these responses and spend time cultivating them, their marriages can be enhanced tremendously. It will take time, but what a reward for the time spent! As Mike Mason wrote in *The Mystery of Marriage,* "There is no work more important than the work of relationship and no relationship more important than one's marriage."[3]

God's Design for Marriage

I want you to understand that Christ is the head of every man, and the man is the head of a woman, and God is the head of Christ (1 Corinthians 11:3).

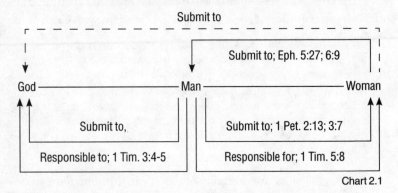

Chart 2.1

To Model Biblical Roles

Not only do we have the responsibility in our marriages to model Christ and the church, but we must also model the roles (job descriptions) God has given us in Scripture. Today's culture wants us to believe men and women are more alike than not. However, even renowned anthropologist and feminist Margaret Mead concluded from her studies that gender role differentiation is a common condition in all cultures.[4]

Let's look at some of the ways men and women are different, and then we'll discuss how their roles differ. This will give us a better understanding of how marriage was intended by God to look and function. This will also help us in later chapters when we look at the potential financial conflicts that can occur within a marriage relationship.

Husband's Job Description

As we saw in the Ephesians passage, a husband is to love his wife but also to be her head. And we read the concept of headship as found in 1 Corinthians 11:3: "I want you to understand that Christ is the head of every man, and the man is the head of a woman, and God is the head of Christ" (see chart 2.1).

The Greek word translated "head" is *kephale*. It means "prime source" or "chief cause." "Headship" means the husband is the prime authority in his family. As God's representative, he provides leadership in the home. He supervises the family and makes sure it's progressing in the right direction. James Dobson, founder of Focus on the Family, points out that "God holds men accountable for leadership in their families. The primary responsibility for provision of authority in the home has been assigned to men."[5]

We see this position of responsibility and headship illustrated clearly in the story of Eli (1 Samuel 2). Eli was married and had two sons. His sons were worthless, and "they did not know the LORD" (verse 12). I find it interesting that they were referred to as "his" sons. This is because Eli was responsible for his family. His wife undoubtedly took part in rearing the boys. But when the time came for God to talk to the family about the boys, it was Eli he talked to and the boys were referred to as "his" sons. God talks specifically to Eli. He doesn't talk to Eli's wife or even to both of them. He sends "a man of God" to declare his judgment to Eli: "This will be the sign to you which will come concerning *your* two sons, Hophni and Phinehas: on the same day both of them will die" (2:34).

In the creation account, we find that "the LORD God formed man of dust from the ground, and breathed into his nostrils the breath of life; and man became a living being" (Genesis 2:7). "Then the LORD God took the man and put him into the garden of Eden to *cultivate* it and *keep* it" (verse 15).

It was in the exercise of *cultivating* that man exhibited one of his responsibilities as the leader of the family—the responsibility of *provision*. He provided through cultivation and working the ground. God says that man would provide all the days of his life, and that it would be hard work (Genesis 3:17-19). Even so, he would still desire to do it. God had put that desire within him so much that even when God cursed the ground, man still cultivated it and worked to provide. Today we see this provision-drive manifested in man's desire and ambition to work (1 Thessalonians 4:11; 2 Thessalonians 3:12). Paul goes so far as to say, "If anyone is not willing to work, then he is not to eat" (2 Thessalonians 3:10).

The word "keep" in Genesis 2:15 refers to *protection*. Man is to protect his wife and family. He is to cover, shield, guard, and defend them. In our society, he does this by buying a house, a dependable car, and insurance. He makes sure his family is clothed and well fed. He puts locks on the doors of his house and takes other steps to ensure his family's safety.

> *God has assigned man the job description to love his wife and to lead her by protecting and providing for her.*

Another way man exercises his role of protector and provider is through his drive to subdue and control his environment. Man was given the mandate by God to subdue the earth and rule over it (Genesis 1:28). Psalm 8 declares that all created things were put in subjection to man: "[O Lord,] what is man that You take thought of him, and the son of man that You care for him?...You make him to rule over the works of Your hands; You have put all things under his feet, all sheep and oxen, and also the beasts of the field, the birds of the heavens and the fish of the sea, whatever passes through the paths of the seas" (verses 4,6-8).

The drive to subdue complements man's drive to provide and protect. The evidence of the drive to subdue is found in his efforts to find cures for diseases, the development of insecticides to control pests, the advances in technology to make work easier, exploring space and landing men on the moon, and so on. Man spends his life trying to subdue his environment, in part to make it easier to provide. When it comes to money, this drive can manifest itself in aggressive investments, long work hours, dedication, and more.

It's very clear that God has assigned man the job description to love his wife and to lead her by protecting and providing for her.

Wife's Job Description

The equally valuable role of helper was given to woman by God because it wasn't good for man to be alone and because he needed a helper (Genesis 2:18). Her job description is defined as companion, helper, and nurturer (2:18; 3:20). To fulfill her job description, a wife's primary responsibilities are *homemaking* and *mothering*. We see this clearly in Scripture:

- Women will be preserved through the bearing of children if they continue in faith and love and sanctity with self-restraint (1 Timothy 2:15).

- I want younger widows to get married, bear children, keep house, and give the enemy no occasion for reproach (5:14).

- [Older women are to] encourage the young women to love their husbands, to love their children, to be sensible, pure, workers at home, kind, being subject to their own husbands, so that the word of God will not be dishonored (Titus 2:4-5).

As a result of her job description, a wife should concentrate first on tasks that fall into the domestic area, such as homemaking and mothering, before getting involved in other areas, including volunteer work and marketplace functions (vocational employment outside the home). We will discuss these areas in chapter 6 by taking a detailed look at Proverbs 31.

Biblical Roles in Harmony

The universal challenge facing men and women is to flesh out and model biblical roles in a world that tells us that being "equal" means "same." More and more, the world tells us we have to blur gender roles. Consider this from Allender and Longman's *Intimate Allies:*

> Gender reflects something about the glory of God. And God's enemy, Satan, wishes to destroy glory. The evil one cannot destroy God; therefore he tries to destroy the reflection of God: man and woman. His prime way of attempting to destroy glory is to make it too frightening to be truly a man or a woman or to offer counterfeit routes to live out gender.[6]

God created us equals as male and female, but He designed us to fulfill unique roles. When these uniquenesses are mixed with money endeavors, conflict can result. (We will look at this in more detail in chapter 3.)

> *If we want ultimate harmony and effectiveness*
> *in our marriages, it's important to put them together*
> *according to God's job descriptions.*

Yes, we can function and our marriages can survive even when we don't order them after God's design. However, if we want ultimate harmony and effectiveness in our marriages, it's important to put them together according to God's job descriptions for us as husbands and wives.

Julie and I have found that it's important for the harmony in our marriage to encourage each other in our unique, God-assigned roles. Without encouragement, our role implementations become more difficult. May God encourage you, and may you encourage each other as you seek Him and manifest biblically based roles in your marriage.

Procreation

Man and woman have a mandate to procreate: "God said to them, 'Be fruitful and multiply, and fill the earth'" (Genesis 1:28). Couples throughout history take this purpose seriously as evidenced by children being continually born. Some couples, however, don't follow through on the responsibility that goes with procreating—the training of the offspring. We're commanded in Scripture to "train up a child in the way he should go, even when he is old he will not depart from it" (Proverbs 22:6). We are also told that we are to teach God's principles diligently to our children as we walk, lie down, get up, and sit in our homes (Deuteronomy 6:6-7). Even with these mandates, too often children's training and well-being is being sacrificed in the pursuit of money and the things it can buy.

In direct relation to our marriage, children are the *only* investment we can make that will last forever. They are the living messages we send to a future time we won't see or experience. Children—not money—are our legacy. And this is the fourth purpose of marriage—godly posterity.

Developing Godly *Posterity*

Except for two letters, the words "prosperity" and "posterity" are the same. Though they sound alike, they are dramatically different in what they mean. Though most of us have probably not stopped to think about the meanings of these words, we pursue one or the other. The way we live our lives demonstrates which of these two is our personal goal.

We all place hope in something of value, profit, gain, or reward to us. For example, when I was in high school, the hope of having my name and picture in the paper (I perceived that to be of value, profit, and reward) was a tremendous source of motivation as I worked out and trained for athletic teams. Hope keeps motivation alive. It incites us to action. You will never be motivated—and thus disciplined—to do anything unless you have hope. The key is in what or in Whom you place your hope.

My observation is that most people are motivated by *prosperity* rather than *posterity*. They are usually driven by the mistaken belief that prosperity means health, wealth, and materialism. This is not the true meaning, as we will see. Even so, with that definition in focus they subtly order their lives around the pursuit of things that God's Word tells us will not last:

[Men's] inner thought is that their houses are forever and their dwelling places to all generations; they have called their lands [and buildings!] after their own names. But man in his pomp will not endure...When he dies he will carry nothing away; his glory will not descend after him. Though while he lives he congratulates himself—and though men praise you when you do well for yourself—he shall go to the generation of his fathers; they will never see the light. Man in his pomp, yet without understanding, is like the beasts that perish (Psalm 49:11-12,17-20).

The futility of pursuing prosperity as defined by money is expressed in Ecclesiastes: "As he had come naked from his mother's womb, so will he return as he came. He will take nothing from the fruit of his labor that he can carry in his hand" (5:15). Prosperity as evidenced by material goods—houses, buildings, and so forth, will not last. Stop and think about that for a minute. The high-rise office building you're in, the mighty fortress you have built as a house, the estate you have amassed—none of it will last.

> *Isn't that something? People define prosperity incorrectly and then pursue it with all they've got.*

So what is the correct definition of prosperity? *Prosperity is simply the state of succeeding in any good and making progress in anything desirable.* In evaluating this definition, we find that wealth and material belongings are really not part of the essence of the definition. Prosperity occurs when someone is making progress in the pursuit and accomplishment of a desirable end. For example, if your goal is to spend two hours a day with your children, you are prosperous as you accomplish that goal. You are prosperous as you do excellent work for your employer. Neither of these situations is directly related to money. Yet you are still prosperous by accomplishing them since they are desired goals for you and in line with what God says are important (Deuteronomy 6:6-8; Colossians 3:23). Earlier, in Joshua 1:8, we read that believers are prosperous and successful if they are doing what God says is important. What does God say should be desirable and important goals?

Your posterity are your descendants. Posterity can also include the other people you influence in ways that may lead to or last through eternity—such as planting a seed about knowing Christ or leading them to salvation. This is how childless couples and single people can also achieve posterity. But if you have children, they are your primary posterity, so throughout this book that's what I will use as the definition of posterity. Psalm 37 reveals a dramatic contrast when it comes to the right kind of prosperity:

> The LORD loves justice and does not forsake His godly ones; they are preserved forever, but the descendants of the wicked will be cut off. The righteous will inherit the land and dwell in it forever (verses 28-29).
>
> Mark the blameless man, and behold the upright; for the man of peace will have a posterity. But transgressors will be altogether destroyed; the posterity of the wicked will be cut off (verses 37-38).

Isn't that something? People define prosperity incorrectly and then pursue it with all they've got, all the while worrying little about the only asset that will last—their posterity. It's quite obvious if we contrast Psalm 49 with Psalm 37 that true prosperity can only be developed through a *righteous* posterity. If our focus isn't on developing godly posterity, we will leave nothing of significance for the generations that come after us. If you give your life to the pursuit of money and the things money can buy and neglect your posterity, you won't leave a lasting, meaningful mark on or for your descendants (or the descendants of the people you've influenced).

> *Posterity will last; prosperity won't.*

I've prepared estate plans for far too many couples who, for various reasons, could not or desired not to leave their hard-earned estates to their children. The reasons ranged from the fact that their children were estranged to the parents not believing their children were trustworthy or competent. These couples had amassed their estates to the exclusion of training and nurturing their offspring. Isn't that an interesting paradox? If we choose to order our lives to leave a posterity, we will have the option to also leave a material estate. However, if the material estate is our focus to the exclusion of posterity, too often we will find that what we have amassed won't matter. Solomon learned this:

> I enlarged my works: I built houses for myself, I planted vineyards for myself; I made gardens and parks for myself and I planted in them all kinds of fruit trees; I made ponds of water for myself from which to irrigate a forest of growing trees...I became great and increased more

than all who preceded me in Jerusalem. My wisdom also stood by me. All that my eyes desired I did not refuse them. I did not withhold my heart from any pleasure, for my heart was pleased because of all my labor and this was my reward for all my labor. Thus I considered all my activities which my hands had done and the labor which I had exerted, and behold all was vanity and striving after wind and there was no profit under the sun...

Thus I hated all the fruit of my labor for which I had labored under the sun, for I must leave it to the man who will come after me. And who knows whether he will be a wise man or a fool? Yet he will have control over all the fruit of my labor for which I have labored by acting wisely under the sun. This too is vanity...

There is nothing better for a man than to eat and drink and tell himself that his labor is good. This also I have seen that it is from the hand of God. For who can eat and who can have enjoyment without Him? For to a person who is good in His sight He has given wisdom and knowledge and joy (Ecclesiastes 2:4-6,18-19,24-25).

I always wonder in the situations of my wealthy clients whether, if given the opportunity to do life over again, they would pursue more balance between their pursuit of accumulating an estate and spending time with their children and training them in the way they should go.

What about *you*? What is your choice going to be? Are you going to spend your time pursuing money (which will not last)? Or will you pursue the development and enhancement of godly posterity and, thus, be truly prosperous? We are free to choose what we will pursue, but we are not free from any consequences of our choices. Posterity will last; prosperity won't.

One Sunday while sitting in church, I ran across an interesting article in a bulletin insert that underscored the importance of focusing on posterity. This article was so personal to me that it sent chills down my spine.

A Sunday school teacher, Ezra Kimball, in 1858 led a Boston shoe clerk to Christ. The clerk, D.L. Moody, became an evangelist, and in 1879 awakened evangelistic zeal in the heart of Frederick B. Meyer, pastor of a small church.

F.B. Meyer, preaching on an American college campus, brought to Christ a student named J. Wilbur Chapman. Chapman engaged in YMCA work, employed a former baseball player, Billy Sunday, to do evangelistic work.

Sunday held a revival in Charlotte, North Carolina. A group of local men were so enthusiastic afterward that they planned another campaign, bringing Mordecai Hamm to town to preach.

In the revival, a young man named Billy Graham heard the Gospel and yielded his life to Christ.[7]

In 1968, at a Billy Graham movie, I became a Christian. A mark left in 1858 is still here in 2012. *I am that mark!* Adding to the awesomeness of this posterity is that Julie's spiritual heritage came through her grandfather, who came to Christ through the influence of Billy Sunday!

Conclusion

I hope you now have a better understanding of the purpose for your marriage. I also pray that you are committed to making it work regardless of the circumstances. Most of all, I encourage you to not allow the pursuit of money (a temporal tool) to destroy your marriage (which can leave an eternal impact through your posterity). The best decision you can make for your posterity (children) is to develop a strong, loving, harmonious marriage.

Game Plan

1. Husbands do you show your wives love in the financial area?

2. Wives, do you truly respect and honor your husbands?

3. What do you think of the definition of prosperity advocated in this chapter?

4. Do you tend to focus more on posterity or prosperity? Explain.

Chapter 3

Reasons for Marriage Conflict

The conflict Rob and Sarah experienced on their trip to Village Crest Inn is typical of many marriages (see introduction). Learning to understand each other and communicate effectively is hard work, and that holds true for this couple. Just as Rob and Sarah need to uncover the reasons for their poor communication, so must we seek the root of our marital conflicts.

"Conflict" can be defined as "strife or contention; to be in opposition one with the other; to be incompatible." As we saw in chapter 2, the purpose of marriage is to live in harmony and unity and develop godly posterity. Isaiah 53:6 gives us some insight into the source of our marital conflict: We want our own way. Although money may appear to be the source of a conflict, all too often it is simply a vehicle through which the real problem will manifest itself. However, in this book we will focus on the financial aspects of conflict.

In the marriage relationship, it's important to understand that men and women perceive money differently. These differences explain in part why money is generally an avenue through which conflict arises. I like what James Dobson says in his book *Love for a Lifetime:*

> Men and women tend to have different value systems which precipitate arguments about money. My father, for example, was a hunter who thought nothing of using three boxes of shotgun shells in an afternoon of recreational shooting. Yet, if my mother spent an equal

amount of money on a "useless" potato peeler, he considered it wasteful. Never mind that she enjoyed shopping as much as he did hunting. They simply saw things differently.[1]

To understand three important areas where these differences are manifested, we'll look at background experiences, temperaments, and basic male/female differences. A clear understanding of these areas as they relate to money will go a long way toward promoting harmony and unity in our marriages.

Background Experiences and Upbringing

As I've worked with couples over the past three decades, I've found that in many cases the conflict over money is because each person came from a different background. Different experiences, family upbringing, and training have caused each spouse to have different expectations of how money is handled.

This was well illustrated by a couple I counseled early in my career. As I talked with them, it became obvious that they disagreed on the use of debt. In going over their net worth statement, I casually asked them the balance owed on their credit cards. When the husband responded that it was "around $8,000," his wife reacted strongly. As I sat there and listened, she went on and on. She said she didn't want to use the credit cards, but he did. And she couldn't understand why he used them so frequently. It made her nervous and upset to use them—and she was equally nervous about *all* the debt they had accumulated.

Needless to say, the husband retaliated with comments of his own. He didn't see any problem using the credit cards since he kept the balance current most months. He also commented that debt was simply a tool to use to grow his net worth. He really didn't see any problem with debt. After all, his father had amassed a small fortune using debt as a tool.

The comment about his father gave me insight into their problem. To see if I was correct, I asked his wife how her family had used debt. She responded they never used it. They always paid cash for everything. As a matter of fact, to her recollection her parents didn't even have a credit card.

Although debt appeared to be the reason for this couple's conflict, in reality their different backgrounds were contributing factors. With our differing backgrounds we bring whole sets of expectations about a wide variety of things into our marriages: how we handle money, how we discipline our children, how we perceive work, how we deal with leisure time, and so forth. With differing expectations comes the potential for conflict.

In *Family. Money.* the authors wrote:

> It has been said that unmet expectations are at the root of all relational conflict...Significant wealth invites a host of expectations. It breeds them. The untapped potential of wealth makes it an endless source of suggestions and possibilities. Inevitably, a handful of those suggestions will solidify into expectations.
>
> The key to resolving and avoiding conflict lies in aligning expectations before they have a chance to develop head-on momentum within the family. Just as expectations are the source of conflict, communication is the key to harmony. And the key to good communication is humility.[2]

The key to overcoming conflict is to make sure good communication takes place between husband and wife. Each person needs to discover what the other's expectations are and then decide what decisions need to be made to promote maximum harmony. In this case, once the husband better understood why his wife always responded to debt the way she did, he was much more sensitive to communicating with her about why he had the debt, what its purpose was, and how it would be repaid.

As you reflect on your own situation, you will undoubtedly find that you and your spouse have different expectations about money, perhaps in areas such as giving, living expenses, and types of investments. You may also find differences in areas such as where you like to go out to eat, shop, or go on vacation. Your spouse may feel uncomfortable in nice restaurants so prefers more middle-of-the-road eating places. Your spouse may like to spend more money on vacations than you do. Vacations may have been emphasized by your spouse's family, while they were really not that big a deal in your family. You may see money used more wisely by purchasing a larger house, while your spouse would rather have a smaller house and newer cars. Differences can go on and on.

We can't change the backgrounds of our spouses, but we can be more sensitive to it so it doesn't contribute to disunity in our marriages. The more in tune we become to our spouses' ideas and the source of them, the greater the mutual understanding and harmony in our marriages. It's essential to communicate to our spouses our expectations about money. We also want to make sure that key financial decisions are made together.

Let me share how Julie and I became aware of the different expectations created by our backgrounds and how we overcame the conflict they caused. Early in our marriage, we had the chance to go to Hawaii on vacation. While we were there, it seemed like we were always at each other's throat. Can you believe that? In a place like Hawaii we were always having a conflict. As a matter of fact, as I reflect, we typically had conflict during all our vacations. Finally, as Julie and I began to talk about it, we realized our views of vacation were totally different.

To me, vacation was getting away and doing nothing. My idea of a vacation was to read a good book and do as little as possible. Julie, on the other hand, looked at vacation as a time to sightsee and do things. Thus, we had conflict because our expectations were so different. Those expectations came in part from our backgrounds. My family did very little on vacation, whereas Julie's family was always on the go. Without realizing it, both of us went on vacation wanting and expecting something different. So what did we do?

We recognized that our expectations wouldn't be a problem if we each gave up our "rights" and "expectations" and, instead, chose to desire above all else that the other person's needs got met. This *is not* a natural, human response, so it didn't come easy. Consequently, we needed to trust God to do it through us. Once we understood the situation, we then communicated clearly about our expectations and decided to enjoy our time together regardless of what we did. Our willingness to submit to each other and relinquish our rights has resulted in some great vacations.

Different Temperaments

Do you remember Rob and Sarah's drive to the Village Crest Inn? Sarah wanted to take a leisurely ride and enjoy and appreciate the scenery, even stopping to take pictures along the way. Rob was a man on a mission. He wanted to get to the inn and start planning. And the sooner the planning was done the better. Obviously they don't have the same God-given temperament.

A key in marriage is understanding that your spouse has a certain temperament, which includes strengths and weaknesses. And the stronger the strengths, the stronger the corresponding weaknesses. Let's define what temperament is and contrast it with character and personality. Temperament expert Tim LaHaye explains:

> *Temperament* is the combination of inborn traits that subconsciously affects man's behavior. These traits are arranged genetically on the basis of nationality, race, sex, and other hereditary factors and are passed on by the genes...*Character* is the real you. The Bible refers to it as the hidden man of the heart. It is the result of your natural temperament modified by childhood training, education and basic beliefs, principles and motivations. *Personality* is the outward expression of ourselves, which may or may not be the same as our character, depending on how genuine we are...In summary, temperament is the combination of traits we were born with; character is our "civilized" temperament; and personality is the "face" we show to others.[3]

Dr. LaHaye cites four basic temperaments: choleric, sanguine, melancholy, and phlegmatic. (See "Characteristics of the Four Temperaments," chart 3.1, on the next page.) Each of us is a mixture of temperaments, but we usually have one that is dominant. It's not important to determine the exact percentages of the mixture but rather to determine the dominant basic temperament you are and understand the associated strengths and weaknesses.

Characteristics of the Four Temperaments

Personality	Choleric	Sanguine	Phlegmatic	Melancholy
Strengths	Leader; optimistic; team player; decisive; adventurous; not easily discouraged; loves a challenge	Warm; lively; fun loving; feelings dominate decisions; compassionate	Good under pressure; witty; dependable; efficient; enjoys humor	Faithful; self-sacrificing; high standard of excellence
Weaknesses	Prone to anger; impetuous; proud; lack of compassion; domineering; blunt	Speaks without thinking; impractical; disorganized; restless; people pleaser; weak willed	Can hurt people with unkind joking; critical; unmotivated; stubborn; indecisive	Self-centered; critical; meddler; moody; overly sensitive; pessimistic
Highest Values	Authority; challenging work; freedom	Recognition; positive environment	Stability; security; team participation; being appreciated	Security; no sudden changes; protection; personal attention

Chart 3.1

Adapted from Tim LaHaye, *Spirit-Controlled Temperament.*

Using the Characteristics of the Four Temperaments chart, we discover that Rob is primarily choleric. He likes to be in charge, is energized by a challenge, and is rarely aware of other people's feelings (including Sarah's). Sarah is primarily phlegmatic. She likes secure situations, is comfortable with the status quo, and needs time to adjust to changes.

Let's look briefly at how these differences might play out in their interactions regarding finances. Rob may not be as concerned about debt as Sarah because he likes the challenge of paying it back, whereas Sarah is concerned because her security orientation is threatened by debt. Another illustration might be a job change. Rob likes the challenge of something new, but Sarah likes the status quo. So even though the job change may result in more money and is a "no brainer" for Rob, Sarah might drag her feet.

Because Rob likes to be in control, he handles the checkbook and asks for little input from Sarah. Sarah wants to be appreciated for having input to offer. Rob is much more likely to be okay with a risky investment than Sarah, who may be reticent to invest.

We'll unpack these differences in more detail as we go through this book, but I'm sure you get the idea. Temperament differences can be a reason for some conflicts about money.

> *Many perceived money problems are not money problems.*
> *Rather, they are problems with understanding*
> *the spouse's temperament.*

When I understand Julie's temperament-based strengths and weaknesses, I can perceive her actions more accurately. Her actions are, in most cases, the result of the God-given tendencies that flow from her temperament, whether they are strengths or weaknesses, and not from ulterior motives. When Julie questions me about a change in our budget, it's not because she's questioning the change but because she wants to have a better understanding of the reason for the change. (She has the same basic temperament I do, so we have a somewhat easier time understanding each other compared to couples who have different temperaments.) Julie wants to know the reason for the change and have some control over the finances as well.

Stop for a moment and think about the different expectations your spouse and you may have based on your inborn temperaments.

The Way We're Wired

As we saw in chapter 2, God has given husbands and wives unique job descriptions and roles. He created us with certain abilities and characteristics physically and emotionally to equip us to do our jobs. He also created us male and female—equal in value but each uniquely designed. So what's so unique about our designs?

> *We need to know the truth about our differences and embrace them as God's means to give us fulfillment and for us to give Him glory.*

As Gary Smalley points out in his book *If Only He Knew*: "The differences (emotionally, mentally, and physically) are so extreme that without a concentrated effort to understand them, it is nearly impossible to have a happy marriage."[4] We live in a world that says if we're equal, we can't be different. Some people say the only differences between male and female are socially induced. But as Mike Mason points out in *The Mystery of Marriage*: "When people forget that the opposite sex is opposite, it can result in men actually resenting women for not being men and vice-versa."[5]

As Christians, we need to know the truth about our differences and embrace them as God's means to give us fulfillment and for us to give Him glory. I remember a phone call I received in college from a friend of mine. He had just been talking with his girlfriend, and he was extremely frustrated that he couldn't get her to see things the way he did. His question to me was "Why doesn't she think like I do?" I couldn't help but laugh as I told him that was quite impossible. She *couldn't* think like he did because she wasn't like him. She never was and never will be.

Not only are we different physically, mentally, and psychologically, but we're different emotionally. Much of the conflict over money occurs in the emotional realm. These emotional differences must be clearly understood to effectively handle them and maximize marital harmony.

Before looking at seven emotional characteristics, let me say that most of us have some of each of the characteristics. Because of the nature of writing a book, I must make sweeping generalities. I know there are an infinite combination of factors that make up each person. It may be that you have more or less of the specific characteristics we'll talk about as a result of your background and temperament. My contention, however, is that gender influences our characteristics. You'll tend toward the characteristics listed for your sex.

1. *Showing love.* Men, for the most part, show love by what they do. Women often interpret love by affection. James Dobson wrote:

> Love is linked to self-esteem in women. For a man, romantic experiences with his wife are warm and enjoyable and memorable—but not necessary. For a woman they are her lifeblood. Her confidence, her sexual response and her zest for living are often directly related to those tender moments when she feels deeply loved and appreciated by her man. That is why flowers and candy and cards are more meaningful to her than to him. This is why she is continually trying to pull him out of the television set or the newspaper, and not vice-versa.[6]

This difference is important to understand as it relates to work and money. One of the reasons many men are motivated to work—even to the exclusion of their families—is that by providing for their families, they feel they're showing love for their wife and children. Although the husband is responsible to provide, he needs to realize that his wife interprets love by the affection he shows, by his communication, and by the time he spends with her.

If couples practice good communication by routinely spending time discussing their day, work, children, goals, disappointments, and dreams, their discussion of finances won't be apt to bring tension. A foundation of love and trust paves the way for healthy interaction.

For more insights into ways husbands and wives show and receive love, I recommend Gary Chapman's book *The Five Love Languages.* Often we give love in the way we'd like to receive it, but it's important to understand the particular "love language" of our spouse.

2. *Identity placement.* The wife often puts her identity in her relationships. She often derives status and worth from her husband, children, and other meaningful relationships. The husband tends to put

his identity in his job. He gets his status and sense of self-worth from it because of his drive to provide.

The different focus of each spouse can obviously lead to conflicts. Since the husband's identity is often tied up in his job and what he can accomplish vocationally, it's easy for him to spend an inordinate amount of time working. When he does this, he tends to damage his relationship with his wife. She may begin to resent his work. Even though he makes more and more money, it doesn't help his relationship with his wife. For her, more money isn't the answer because her identity isn't in the money but in her relationship with him. She wants him to be home and part of her life. (In chapter 4 we'll unpack in more detail how this difference manifests itself in the work arena.)

3. *Tolerance for risk.* This is a big one. Since the man is responsible to provide, he tends to have a greater tolerance for risk and rejection. He has to be more comfortable taking risks because it's risky to go out into the marketplace to provide, to subdue and conquer his environment, and to protect his territory. There are constant challenges for him to face and overcome in his role as provider. Someone else may take his job, so he needs to keep his skills up; a competitor may move into his space; his biggest client may play hardball with him regarding his fees; and so on. He must have the emotional makeup to handle these and many other challenges.

> *With the risk-taking bent often comes a less-worried viewpoint.*

The woman, on the other hand, has the primary responsibility to nurture. With that responsibility often comes the desire to be secure. It's difficult to nurture and raise a family without the security of a home and a fixed income. This is why it's much more difficult for a woman to move out of the home for a job change than for the husband. To him it's "just a move." To her it is leaving a place of security, a place where she has invested energy and put down roots.

Let's consider some other manifestations of this difference in the financial realm. If the husband wants to start a new vocation with uncertain income and leave a vocation with a fixed income, who is usually more hesitant? The wife. Who is more willing to take the risk of an aggressive investment? The husband. Who tends to want to make sure the budget is working and that there is enough money to meet even unexpected emergencies? The wife. Who tends to be most comfortable with the use of debt as a tool? The husband.

One more thing about this difference: With the risk-taking bent often comes a less-worried viewpoint. With the security orientation comes the tendency to worry. A man typically doesn't worry too much about events. A woman sees them in a more personal, attached way. She tends to be more subjective and feelings oriented.

This difference in the tendency to worry is seen very clearly when the husband loses his job. The wife may worry and wonder why her husband doesn't seem concerned. He's not worried because he knows he'll get another job and provide for his family. The same thing happens if an investment goes bad. The husband's response is typically, "That's the way it goes. It's part of the game." The wife, on the other hand, may worry about what the loss means for the future.

4. *Sensitivity level.* Men tend to be more insensitive, and women tend to be more sensitive. This is a result of the man being more thing-centered and idea-centered. He's more concerned about projects, abstract principles, and getting the job done than he is about *how* he gets the job done and perhaps even the feelings of the people involved in doing the job. His need to provide may cause him to be this way. He leans toward justice and strictness. The woman, on the other hand, is more people-centered and concerned about the process of getting things done. She is more tuned into the human side of things and tends to be more merciful and lenient.

This difference can manifest itself in many different ways financially. Regarding bill paying, the husband could be less sensitive to being delinquent on some of the monthly bills than the wife. To him it's no big deal if a vendor needs to wait a couple more days. The wife tends to always want to be current because other people are involved. In the charitable giving area, the wife's sensitivity could cause her to be more inclined to give to a need than the husband. Requests for money tend to pull on the heartstrings, and the wife will typically be more sensitive to the need.

This leads to another difference. In most cases, men are slower to show emotion than women. To a large degree, this is a function of the sensitivity quotient…or lack thereof. This is why women may be upset enough to cry if the checkbook doesn't balance or there isn't enough money to pay the bills. Men may get upset too, but they won't show it. As a matter of fact, they may come across as indifferent, which can compound the problem. She can't understand why he seems oblivious, and that frustrates her even more.

Since money is such a potentially emotional area of a couple's life, it's important they have a plan to handle the ups and downs. The plan needs to be designed to reduce emotional strain primarily on the wife, since she tends to be more emotional. (In chapter 12, we'll look at the plan Julie and I have used for more than 30 years.)

5. *Need for encouragement.* Since men have the responsibility to provide, and since they often take risks to do so, they need to be encouraged. Their greatest ego need is to have a continual vote of confidence, to be honored, and to be respected.

One of the reasons husbands sometimes work long hours is because they get their ego needs met at work. The wife can help meet this need by telling her husband that he's doing a good job, that she's proud of him. Failure to do so may result in extra-long work hours, or he could react the opposite way and become slothful because he feels unappreciated.

A wife who intentionally builds up her spouse will likely have a husband who is enthusiastic and secure about his role as provider. A wife who doesn't encourage her husband in his role or who is constantly confronting him because he doesn't make enough money, may drive him to make risky investments, take on excessive debt, or change jobs unwisely to try to succeed in her eyes and gain her approval and respect. These actions go in the opposite direction of what she really wants—security, stability, and minimal risk.

Likewise, a wife typically needs to be encouraged in her role as helper and partner. Since she tends to be more loving, more emotional, more subjective, and more dependent, she's more subject to loneliness. This loneliness exacerbates her need for a close interpersonal relationship and heart-to-heart communication with her husband. She wants to talk with him and have him value her input. This is why involving her in the budget process is so important. It affirms her. This is what Sarah was trying to tell Rob. Her input on the couple's investments was also critical. Not only will she be encouraged as she gives input but an added benefit is that her intuitive ability is typically a good source of counsel in the decision-making process.

Particular encouragement is needed if the wife is also a mom. Child-rearing is such a long-term job that moms need to be encouraged to persevere. I believe that some wives and moms, though not desiring to leave their children, go back into the workplace to get positive support and encouragement because they're not getting it from their husbands. Men, if we want to leave godly posterity, we need to encourage our wives in their valuable roles.

6. *Long-term v. short-term thinking.* Because of the provision responsibility, it's not uncommon for men to tend to have a longer time horizon than women. Men tend to see the big picture and look down the road. They are generally more concerned about retirement than women. This is also one of the reasons men tend to handle long-term investments that aren't easily converted into cash, such as real estate, better than women do.

If it takes 10 to 15 years to get money out of the investment, most women usually aren't too interested. She tends to focus on the present. This perspective is necessary for her because she has the responsibility of nurturing. She has to deal with the short-term needs of the family. While he's thinking retirement and education, she's thinking groceries and shoes for the kids.

This difference makes it obvious how much we need each other. The short term and the long term are both important in a couple's financial life. Long-term plans must be made, but not at the expense of short-term needs. Harmony is enhanced in the marriage as husband and wife realize that both of their perspectives are needed, and they make financial decisions together.

7. *Logical v. intuitive.* All couples who have been married know this difference exists, though it is likely many can't explain it. The husband tends to like facts and will analyze every detail of a financial opportunity. Meanwhile, the wife comes to a conclusion without really understanding how she reached it. She just seems to "sense" the situation.

How this difference manifests can cause much frustration. The husband can spend hours analyzing, sorting, and calculating the return on investment (ROI), only to have his wife give a definitive response in a matter of seconds. His normal response to her quick view or decision is one of bewilderment. "How can she say that? She doesn't have the facts." His natural tendency then is to discount what she's said. This reduces her feeling of importance and value, which causes strain on the relationship. The truth is that her God-given intuition is just as important as the facts.

The wife, on the other hand, may have a hard time understanding why her husband has to go through all the calculations and analysis to come to a decision. She can get to the conclusion without all the detail and hassle. The key is to allow each spouse to exercise his or her bent (logic or intuition), and for both to be given equal credibility when it comes to making decisions. (We'll see this difference at work in chapter 10 regarding investments.)

Conclusion

In summary, we've seen that conflict can be influenced by different backgrounds, different temperaments, and an unclear understanding of basic male/female differences. As we'll see in the remainder of this book, one, two, or all three of these areas may be causing conflict over money in your marriage. My hope is that your increased understanding of these areas will help you overcome any money conflicts you face.

Game Plan

1. Do you and your spouse have different financial backgrounds? In what ways?

2. Do you and your spouse have different temperaments? Explain.

3. Do you agree with the basic male/female differences Russ outlined? Why or why not?

4. Do you know your temperament? Have you taken a personality or temperament test? If you'd like to, please see some recommended tests and their web addresses in the end notes.[7]

Chapter 4

Work: Blessing or Curse?

Much conflict in marriage is the result of incorrect thinking about work. Conflict can result when the husband works too much or not enough (see chapter 5). Another source of conflict can be when the wife works vocationally outside the home (see chapter 6).

Why does a husband work too much or not at all? What causes a wife and mother to go outside the home to work? Before we explore the specifics, we first need to gain an understanding of God's design for work. We will then have a proper view of our income.

Work Defined

Work can be defined as the physical and mental energy exerted and directed to some end or purpose. For our discussion, I will define work to mean "vocational employment for the purpose of generating income to provide for the family." Since work is tied to provision, and provision is primarily the husband's responsibility, my remarks throughout this chapter are directed specifically to the husband. These principles, however, also apply to wives who must work vocationally to provide for their families. The following basic tenets will help focus our thoughts.

1. *Man has a God-given drive to provide, and as a result, he works.*

> Now no shrub of the field was yet in the earth, and no plant of the field had yet sprouted, for the Lord God had not sent rain upon the earth, and there was no man to cultivate the ground...Then the Lord God took the man and put him into the Garden of Eden to cultivate it and keep it (Genesis 2:5,15).

The desire to work flows from man's drive to provide.

2. As a result of his work, the husband generates income for the purpose of meeting the needs of his family.

> If anyone does not provide for his own, and especially for those of his household, he has denied the faith and is worse than an unbeliever (1 Timothy 5:8).
>
> Even when we were with you, we used to give you this order: if anyone is not willing to work, then he is not to eat, either (2 Thessalonians 3:10).

Why Do We Work?

We work for several reasons. First, *man works because work is good.* Work is valued by God. We see in Genesis 1 that what God did in the creation of the world was good—very good. We also see that work is good because we're in partnership with God regarding it. God planted the garden and put man in it to cultivate it (Genesis 2:5,15). We work because we have the incredible privilege of co-laboring with God. The psalmist revealed this co-laboring when he wrote, "[O Lord,]You make him to rule over the works of Your hands; You have put all things under his feet" (Psalm 8:6). God allows us to assist Him in the management of creation. We work, then, because of the great dignity God affords us as His co-laborers. Work is a gift from God (Ecclesiastes 5:18-19).

Many people wrongly believe that work is a result of the curse given after Adam and Eve's disobedience. But God cursed the *ground* as a result of the fall of man. He didn't curse the task of working. Work has indeed become harder to accomplish as a result of the fall, but it still remains a good and proper activity. Although Solomon teaches that all labor is "vanity" or useless, work is still to be undertaken and even enjoyed (see the book of Ecclesiastes). The frustration we experience as we toil is balanced by the joy of accomplishment and the provision our work produces.

Second, *we work because Scripture commands us to.* As noted earlier, if a man does not work, he is not to eat (2 Thessalonians 3:10). If a man is slothful, he may fail to provide for his family and become a bad testimony and witness of the Lord to his family and to the world. He also runs the risk of seeing the marriage roles reversed as his wife takes on the provision responsibility that really belongs to him. With role reversal comes the potential for disharmony in the marriage.

> *Retirement to a life of leisure is dangerous.*

Third, *we work because the process of working is a significant means of fulfillment.* A man is fulfilled when he works because that's how God created him. The God-given drive to provide carries with it a God-given desire to work. In my consulting role, I've had the opportunity to work with many individuals who have "arrived" financially. They have millions of dollars from selling a business, wealth accumulation over time, inheritances, and so on. Whatever the source of their money, they're in a position to never again need to work in an income-generating vocation. You would think they would be fulfilled, content, and happy, but in many cases they are not. Many of them told me, "Russ, I have got to get back to work! This doing nothing is driving me crazy. I can only play so much golf, and I'm tired of it!"

This is why retirement to a life of leisure is dangerous. It takes away the fulfillment an individual derives from working and being productive. I'm not saying we can't change the form of our work, but we are most fulfilled if we stay productive even if it's in a volunteer capacity.

Fourth, *we work because it gives us an environment for living the Christian life, sharing our faith in Christ, and growing spiritually with other believers.* Christianity is not meant to be just a part of a person's life. It should be so central that it overflows into *every aspect* of our lives, especially our work. Our ultimate purpose as believers is fulfilled because the workforce marketplace gives us unique and challenging opportunities to fulfill our God-given responsibility of being salt and light, sharing Christ, and growing as believers.

Fifth, *we work because it is an avenue God gives us to provide for our families.* We can easily conclude incorrectly that our abilities or intellects enable us to provide. Scripture, however, makes it clear that work is simply the *vehicle* of our provision. God is the source (Deuteronomy 8:16-18; Proverbs 10:22).

Though income is a result of our work (the product), it shouldn't be our pursuit. If we focus on the product (income) rather than the *process*, we can experience frustration and lack of fulfillment. After all, everything we produce will ultimately be burned up (2 Peter 3:10). Solomon realized the futility of focusing on the product of his labor. He wrote, "[Man] will take nothing from the fruit of his labor that he can carry in his hand" (Ecclesiastes 5:15).

> *Your responsibility is to work hard and excellently at what God has called and equipped you to do, realizing that the income you generate is determined by Him and is His responsibility.*

If we pursue money, it takes wings like an eagle and flies away (Proverbs 23:4-5). Though money has utilitarian value (we use it to buy things to meet our needs), it has no long-term, intrinsic value because it won't last. It is thus vain to focus on it. Another reason we can be frustrated if we focus on income is that we will constantly be evaluating our worth and success on the basis of what we earn in comparison to others. As we discussed in chapter 1, such a comparison is futile because the income we earn is in God's hands and has nothing to do with whether or not we personally are successful.

If we pursue income as the sole purpose of working, our lives will be marked by that focus. We'll end up working longer hours, forgetting that working more hours doesn't always guarantee more income. We will become competitive, anxious, unsatisfied, self-centered wealth seekers who always measure what we do by the product of our work.

The key truth about work can be summed up this way: Your responsibility is to work hard and excellently at what God has called and equipped you to do, realizing that the income you generate is determined by Him and is His responsibility (Colossians 3:23-24). God is more concerned about the *process* of your working than He is about the product of your work. Tremendous freedom can result if you grasp and live by this awesome principle.

If you find yourself thinking that your income isn't fair or that it doesn't seem right that another person earns more than you do, you may not have the correct perspective on work. Regard those thoughts as a warning indicator and respond by spending more time with God and His Word to gain His perspective on your income and perception of work. If you don't, your work could get out of balance and cause stress on your marriage.

Finding Balance

So far we've discovered that God has equipped men to fill different vocational jobs. Man is responsible to work hard and excellently at his job, and the resulting income is in God's hands. Within the "working hard and excellently" phrase is an implied *balance*. It stands to reason that if our income is in God's hands, He will meet our needs without our overworking. This is verified in Psalm 127:2: "It is vain for you to rise up early, to retire late, to eat the bread of painful labors; for He gives to His beloved even in his sleep." Proverbs 10:22 says, "It is the blessing of the LORD that makes rich, and He adds no sorrow to it."

> *The boundary lines between work time and family time have become blurred.*

Charles Deems, a nineteenth-century writer noted, "All men must work, but no man should work beyond his physical and intellectual ability, nor beyond the hours which nature allots. No net result of good to the individual nor the race comes of any artificial prolonging of the day at either end. Work while it is day. When night comes, rest."[1]

What is our allotted time to work? If our marriage relationship is important and our children are important, we need to build time in our days to spend with family in addition to the time we spend working. All too often our families get "leftover" time. Julie and I have found that by scheduling in time with the family (meals, sporting events, vacations, and so forth), we then know what is left for work. If we don't build in this family time, work time tends to expand and fill up our days.

The boundary lines between work time and family time have become blurred. This is especially a problem today with so many people working from home and telecommuting. Intentional scheduling of our time at least gives us a shot at finding balance in our lives and puts a governor on overworking. "Overwork" can be defined as "a prolonged state of working exceedingly long hours to the exclusion of other priority areas in your life." One way to determine if this is a problem area for you is to ask your spouse. Julie was a really good checkpoint for me on this.

The stakes are high when it comes to balance. For those who allow their lives to become unbalanced by leaning heavily toward work, consider 1 Timothy 6:9: "Those who want to get rich fall into temptation and a snare and many foolish and harmful desires which plunge men into ruin and destruction." This ruin and destruction could be in the forms of a rocky marriage, undisciplined kids, and bad business deals. If you remain confident God will meet your income needs, you will experience more freedom in your work because you realize your part is to do what you can in the allotted work time and trust God to do what you can't do.

I've found that a couple of changes in the way a husband and wife think can make this balancing act somewhat easier to attain. The first is to not be in a hurry to quit working. If you have extra funds and can put them aside for retirement, fine. But to focus on retirement puts additional stress on the family. As we've already seen, retirement from production to leisure is difficult for a man and not a worthy goal.

When you realize you have your entire lifetime to accumulate, you can experience more balance and enjoy the trip. Twelve to 15-hour days of work to the exclusion of your family so you can "arrive" or "retire" isn't wise. And in the long run, it won't be profitable.

The second area of thinking to consider is understanding that overworking to accumulate a financial estate to pass on to your children, without spending time training your children, may backfire. If your posterity haven't been trained in money matters, they may not be able to wisely handle a generous inheritance. If you don't spend time training them and acting as a role model for them, it will be very difficult for them to learn the truths you want them to learn, especially about money. I think it's a travesty when I meet someone who has worked his entire life and amassed a fortune and he tells me, "Russ, I really can't leave this to my children because they can't handle it." This is why the development of godly posterity is so critical. You must spend *time* with your children to train them. Don't get to the end of your life and say, as Solomon did, that all was vanity because you focused on money instead of your posterity (Ecclesiastes 2:20-22).

To find out whether your perspective of work is long-term, and whether you have good balance, ask yourself these questions:

- Can I leave my work at the office?
- Can I relax?
- Can I sleep?
- Am I anxious?
- Is my self-image tied directly to my job?
- Do I measure how I'm doing by comparing myself to the other guy?

Your answers to these questions will help you understand your view of work and its place in your life. If you can sleep, relax, enjoy what you're doing, and have a good self-image apart from your job, you probably have a proper understanding of why you work and Who is the ultimate source of your income. If you find yourself able to spend time with your family, enjoy vacations, and really know your children, you probably have good balance when it comes to work and family life.

Determining Your Vocation

Throughout this chapter I've said that you should do what God has called you to do. To determine your job calling, consider these factors:

- Are you equipped for the vocation?
- Is the vocation worthwhile?
- Do you enjoy the work?

Are you equipped for the job? God doesn't call us to a vocation for which we are not equipped. Therefore, in evaluating your vocational calling, look at the God-given resources you have (temperament, experience, background, training); look at your options and opportunities; look at your feelings, desires, and motivation; and then choose a job based on those factors, matching your abilities as closely as possible with the vocation.

Is the vocation worthwhile? Any job is worthwhile if it makes a positive contribution to people. Whether you're a computer tech, a grocer, an electrician, a teacher, a doctor, whatever, practically everything a person does vocationally is worthwhile to society. The way you make a contribution to people through your vocation is to focus on them as you perform your work. In other words, be sensitive to the needs around you in the marketplace. Focus not on the income but rather on the way you do your work.

Do you enjoy the work? Solomon makes it very clear that we're meant to *enjoy* our labor. "Labor is a gift of God" and "nothing is better than that man should be happy in his activities, for that is his lot" (Ecclesiastes 3:13,22). This doesn't mean work is easy or that it will always be exciting or interesting. In fact, we're told that work will be hard (Genesis 3:19). Yes, hard, but for the most part, also enjoyable. Typically, this is most easily accomplished when we match up our gifts, temperaments, and abilities with our vocations.

Changing Vocations

If you're working hard and excellently at the vocation God has equipped you for and you have work in proper perspective, is there ever a time you would change jobs? Yes, there might be. Motivation is the critical key. And your motivation shouldn't simply be to make more money. If someone changes jobs *only* to make more income, he will forever be frustrated because income isn't a true source of fulfillment. The person who seeks more income typically goes from job to job and remains unsatisfied.

Job changes should come from the desire and need to better fulfill our life purpose. This presupposes, of course, that each of us is already fulfilling his God-given purpose in his current vocation. The key is to be involved in God's purpose where you are. Then, if *He* wants you to change jobs to better fulfill your life purpose, He will open the way. Income considerations should be secondary.

Conclusion

We've focused on two crucial issues that go together: work and income. Here is a summary of the key points from a biblical perspective:

- God has called and equipped a man to work as a means of providing for his family.
- Work is good. In order for a man to be most fulfilled, he will want to work at something productive.
- Man is to work excellently at his vocation with the realization that the income generated is ultimately God's decision and in His hands.
- Since the income and assets a man accumulates from his work will be left to those who come after him, he is wise to train his posterity.
- Since this training takes time, a man should make sure early on that his life is ordered by *time* priorities, not *income* priorities, and that he has good balance between work and family in his life.
- In the process of working, a man should focus on people rather than on his income.
- A man should view his work as a place where he can share his faith and reach the world for Christ.
- Job changes should occur to allow a man to better fulfill his life purpose, not just to make more money.

I encourage you to evaluate your purpose in working, your work habits, your life priorities, and your short- and long-term goals. Not only can you revolutionize your present life and have more harmony in your marriage by bringing your thoughts of work and income in line with God's Word, but you will impact future generations for Christ.

Game Plan

1. Is your home life and work life in good balance? Why or why not?

2. Do you enjoy your work?

3. Have you ever changed vocations? Why did you change?

4. Do you use your job as a platform to share Christ?

Part 2

8 Important Decisions

Chapter 5

Will He Ever Come Home?

After a good night's sleep, our friends Sarah and Rob were ready to tackle the packet with their name on it that they found in their room at the Village Crest Inn. Even though Rob preferred doing something outside, he knew this "planning weekend" was needed in their marriage. He'd looked ahead in the notebook and realized the decisions to be discussed over the next couple of days were ones that needed to be talked about. They had always stuck to the periphery of these decisions in their talks, but he had never addressed them in detail with Sarah. He was looking forward to the discussion. Quite frankly, he did want to have less conflict with Sarah, especially when it came to money.

Decision 1: How Much Should We Work?

Sarah couldn't believe the issue highlighted as Decision 1. Earlier that week she had excitedly prepared for a leisurely Mexican dinner with their friends the Carters. Rob and Sarah hadn't visited with them for months. Sarah had set the table with brightly colored plates and festive napkins she'd found on sale. Even though she didn't work outside the home, between school meetings, church, and sports activities, Sarah kept busy and had little down time. This evening would be a welcome reprieve—and would include actual adult conversation! Now Sarah recalled the exchange that occurred between Rob and her that night.

Just as she was pulling the enchiladas out of the oven, the phone rang. It was Rob. "Sarah, I think you'll have to start without me," Rob said. "We've run into a problem here."

"But, honey, the Carters will be here any minute!" Sarah said. "Isn't it something that can wait?"

"Well, technically it could wait," Rob said. "But this is a chance to look really good in front of my boss. You know I have my review coming up, so I really think I need to stay."

"But this is the third night this week," Sarah said. "And you also went to the office the past two weekends. Is this ever going to end? When will you spend time with the children and me?"

"Sarah, I really don't know!" Rob responded. "You know I'm doing this for you and the kids. How do you think everything gets paid for anyway? Go ahead without me. I'll be there as soon as I can."

When Sarah and Rob sat down to tackle Decision 1, Rob also remembered the incident with Sarah the night of the dinner party. He recalled his angry words to Sarah when she hadn't been very supportive of his need to work late. He'd slammed down the phone after talking to her, but he also knew Sarah was right. He had been overworking, and it was time they talked about it. How much he was working and what he was doing had come about by default. His work time had gradually increased without conscious awareness. And Sarah's activities had also seemed to just happen. Did they need to adjust what they were doing? As Rob thought about what he'd said to Sarah on the phone, he wondered why he'd really been working so much. Was it just to gain his boss's approval or was there more to it?

Reasons for a Man to Overwork

Every man who is conscientious in his drive to provide for his family will be inclined to work…and work hard. *A man may overwork because of his God-given drive to provide,* sometimes even to the detriment of his family. Thus, a man's provision-drive taken to an extreme becomes a negative factor rather than a positive one. A husband can spend so much time providing that he doesn't spend time with those for whom he is providing. He accumulates prosperity by the world's definition to the exclusion of dealing with his posterity.

Husbands are called to provide not just money for their families but also themselves.

Granted, at times men can be slothful and aren't properly exercising their drive to provide, but it's been my observation that in most cases a man tends to work too much rather than too little. A man's provision drive often causes him to pursue financial independence as quickly as he can. This desire to be independent isn't the problem; rather, the problem is the short time frame in which he tries to accomplish this. I've consulted with many men who believe they should be millionaires by the time they hit 40 to be considered successful. They forget that work is normative, and that they should expect to do it their entire lives. This desire to be wealthy as soon as possible can lead to very unwise decisions regarding family and other priorities.

Again, the key is balance. The husband must realize that if he doesn't pay special attention to the needs of his wife and children, primarily by spending time with them, all his pursuits and long-term endeavors, however noble, will result in hollow victories. Husbands are called to provide not just money for their families but also themselves. A husband needs to show up!

A man may overwork because his needs are not being met at home. Three of man's greatest needs are to be respected, honored, and supported by their wives. If a husband doesn't have these needs met at home, he'll try to get them at the office. Thus, overworking could become the norm. He feels better about himself at work than at home, so why go home?

I love it when Julie tells me I'm the best at what I do. I'm always most encouraged when she tells me how much she appreciates what I do vocationally. It makes me smile when she tells me she thinks I'm the greatest provider in the world and she's continually amazed at what I know about finances. She not only believes I do my job well, but she also tells me so. Wow! Her comments give me great confidence and fulfillment. I know I'm successful in her eyes as she communicates her honor and respect for me. I would do anything for her. When my day is done, I want to be with her. I don't want to spend too much time at work because it takes away time I could be spending with her. Wives who are quick to respect, honor, and support their husbands will have men who want to come home. A friend of mine summed up how important this is when he said, "I can handle anything as long as I know my wife is behind me and supporting me in what I do."

This brings me to another important need men have: *peace at home*. I know I can do a better job at work knowing Julie is managing the home front and peace exists there. I think most husbands would say the same.

When Julie was working as a certified nurse anesthetist (CRNA) right after we were married, everything went well initially. But as her time at work gradually increased and her time at home got shorter, the situation became frustrating. Time for meals together were missed, keeping the house clean and orderly was difficult, and Julie's emotional energy was split. The chaos increased with the addition of children, making peace at home even more elusive. Julie and I wanted a well-ordered home as well as more time to spend together. After discussion, we decided the solution for us was for her to stop working outside the home.

Wives, if you're actively involved outside the home—either in your vocation, hobbies, or volunteer activities—are you able to meet this need for peace at home?

A husband may be working long hours because his focus is misplaced. He may be concentrating on generating more income as a measure of success. Men can easily reason that long work hours are a small price to pay for the prestige and power money brings on a worldly level. His identity is in his job. The only problem is that the power and prestige don't give him what he needs. What he really wants is a meaningful purpose, a good self-image, and to love and be loved. Overworking does not provide those things.

The best investment is usually not the flashiest. Your posterity fits that description. Gordon MacDonald writes, "Like the fledgling company, a child seems so small, nondescript, and easy to handle with minimum concern. But big returns never happen in the future unless *sizable investments* are made in the present...Is there a price to be paid? Unquestionably! And it is paid right up front, at the beginning of the child's life; the returns come much later."[1] Many don't understand this or they're unwilling to pay that price. Men, how many investments can you make that pay eternal dividends? Don't let the amazing and seemingly short-lived opportunities of investing in your children's lives when they are young slip through your fingers.

A man may work long hours in pursuit of position. A man may be climbing the ladder in pursuit of a position in his company or profession because he wants to "be somebody" among his peers. Did you notice I said "a position"? Therein lays the fallacy of this pursuit. "Position" can be defined as a person's standing in relation to another person. This means he has to be looking horizontally at how he is doing to compare himself with those around him. As Christians, we're not to compare ourselves with one another. We're to look vertically, *focusing only on God.* And then we do the very best work we can in an excellent manner (Colossians 3:23).

This means that "position" should not be our focus because in this lifetime we will never fully "arrive" at the "top." We're all in a process called life that is ongoing. Any position we hold at a given point has been determined by God. And it usually changes as we continue on living. How unsettling and futile it would be to focus on working long hours to arrive at a position that at best is only temporary. We need to seek God, work hard, relax, and enjoy the *process* of living.

A husband may overwork because he perceives his wife isn't satisfied. A while back some friends invited us over for dinner. The husband asked me what I thought about a new job he expected to be offered. It involved more money but also required a minimum of three nights away from home each week. I told him he should think through his goals regarding family and income and carefully weigh the pros and cons before making the decision. If he didn't take the time to seriously think it over and pray about it, the lure of more income could appear so attractive that he might take the job by overlooking some of the negatives. Money has a way of clouding our thinking, even on really important issues. About six months later we heard from this man's wife. He had taken the job, and now she was frustrated because he was always traveling. She was concerned because their children were growing up without their father.

As Julie and I discussed the situation, she reminded me of some comments the wife had made prior to her husband's taking the job. She'd indicated to Julie that she wasn't happy with the carpet in their house and that she was "sick and tired" of driving their current car. She didn't want to entertain at home until they did some remodeling, and she couldn't understand why her husband wouldn't give her the money to do that. It was very clear to Julie that one of the reasons her husband had been motivated to take the job was his wife's subtle-yet-incessant demands for more money. He probably felt the best way he could get his wife what she wanted—to provide for her—was to work more.

We heard later that the switch in jobs started a cycle of the husband changing jobs to make more money, which required more work time, and resulted in less and less time with his wife and kids.

A Wife's Response to Her Husband's Overworking

A wife might have several responses to the long hours her husband works. *Her first response may be a general feeling of being unfulfilled.* A wife is fulfilled when she engages in conversation, affection, honesty, and openness with her husband. If he's working long hours, it's difficult for him to have the time necessary to communicate effectively and wholeheartedly with his wife. Dr. Willard F. Harley, a veteran marriage counselor, recommends that couples spend at least 15 hours a week together—excluding sleeping and eating. If a husband is working long hours, finding 15 hours will be difficult.

> *Long days should not become the norm because of the negative impact on the family.*

Is it any wonder that many times men who get their fulfillment at the office find their wives seeking fulfillment in their children, church, social activities, or a job outside the home? Here's the irony. The very thing a wife wants—time with her husband—she may jeopardize because she expresses discontent with his income. By wanting more money or possessions, she subtly pressures him to work more. In the end, she may end up having more money but losing what she values most—time with him.

A wife may feel unloved if her husband is overworking. A woman is usually very relationship centered. She yearns to be a companion to the one she loves. But if her husband is never home and doesn't take the time to show his appreciation for all she does, it's difficult for her to feel she's worthwhile and successful in fulfilling her role. She may conclude that it's futile to try to please her husband because his work is obviously more important to him than she is.

I remember early on in my financial planning career working 12- to 14-hour days. Julie became frustrated and told me she felt unimportant because of the hours I was putting in at work. (Women spell love t-i-m-e.) Although I wasn't verbally telling her she was less important to me than my work, my actions were saying it.

Since that time, I've realized that it's important not to allow my work to take precedence over my wife. This isn't to say there aren't occasional long-hour days. There will be, and a man needs to have the freedom to work hard and occasionally put in long days to meet the needs of his employer. Long days should not, however, become the norm because of the negative impact on the family.

Through long and short days I make the effort to stay tuned in to Julie and focused on her need to be at the forefront of my thinking. Over the years I've communicated this in different ways. One day I went home for lunch (a 30-minute drive) and took her some flowers. This surprise made the statement that even though I spent a lot of hours at work, she was my number one priority. I also send cards to Julie when I travel on extended business trips. I mail them so she'll get one each day I'm gone. (Men, since we can so easily put our identity in our jobs, we must be quick and creative in communicating to our wives that we value them more than our work.)

A wife may respond to her husband's overworking by nagging him to spend more time at home. We see in Scripture that a contentious wife is like a dripping faucet (Proverbs 27:15). Needless to say, nagging adds to the difficulty in building harmony. The backlash is that often the husband works more so he doesn't have to listen to the nagging.

Solutions to Overworking

What are some answers to conflicts around working too many hours? Here are some thoughts to consider.

- The husband and wife need to have a clear understanding of work. They need to recognize that their income level is a *function* of the husband's vocation and isn't necessarily dependent on working a greater number of hours. The harmony in your marriage will be enhanced as these truths are worked out in your situation.

- A wife needs to seek to understand the drive her husband has to provide. She must be careful not to tear it down by nagging at him; rather, she should encourage him in this role of provider. If a husband feels his wife is content with his income, he will be less likely to overwork. It will be easier for him to settle into an allotted time frame for work.

- Overworking should be the exception rather than the norm. There may be times when a man must put in extra hours in the short term. Starting a new job, changing positions in his current company, learning a new skill, meeting a project deadline, or taking a second job for a specific purpose may require additional work time.

  The key is that over any extended period of time (six months to a year), you should be able to observe movement toward achieving or maintaining good balance in your life. Too often men extend the available period for change over their entire working lifetime. They keep telling their wives that next year it will be better, but the balance never comes. Wives need to be prepared for some late nights, but again, these should be the exception.

- If the husband continues to exhibit a pattern of overworking, both the husband and the wife need to consider the possible reasons. Does the husband have a misplaced focus? Has he made an idol of work? Has the wife exhibited a spirit of discontentment that is driving him to work more? Does the husband want more earthly treasures?

Conclusion

Yes, it's important for men to work hard to provide for their families, but we need to be careful not to neglect our wives and children. We need to strive to keep a positive balance in our lives when it comes to work and family. If leaving godly posterity (your children) is your goal, you need to have time to do other things in your life besides work. It's critical for you to develop priorities that enable you to build your posterity even while you're engaged in earning a living. Your children need you *now* not next year. They need *you*, not a substitute. Author Tim Hansel explains:

> The home is the single most important influence on my family. I can delegate a lot of my responsibilities at work, but I cannot delegate my hopes for my family. The primary values, attitudes, skills, and competencies that my children will grow up with will be learned (or not learned) in my home.
>
> Time is the very crucible of fathering. The most profound way I let my family know I love them is by giving them time.
>
> A father is a man who is honest enough to realize that his responsibilities must determine his priorities.[2]

A harmonious marriage is a key contributor to leaving a godly posterity, and achieving that is only possible through the investment of significant quantities of *time*. Spending time together consistently over the months and years is vital. To do this, work and other interests, such as fishing, golfing, and hobbies, must be kept in balance with family time.

Every couple must wrestle with their priorities and how much the husband is going to work. This is a difficult decision, but God will give you wisdom as you work together to create a balance that works for you. "If any of you lacks wisdom, let him ask of God, who gives to all generously and without reproach, and it will be given to him" (James 1:5).

Game Plan

1. Husbands and dads, are you as zealous about training your children as you are about work?

2. What are you doing to intentionally build values and character into the next generation?

3. Do you struggle with overworking? Explain.

4. Is balance a worthwhile pursuit? Is it possible to achieve in today's society?

5. How does a person keep from becoming slothful? Is work a good antidote for that?

Chapter 6

The Myth of the Working Mother

As Rob and Sarah thought about the questions in the notebook from the packet, they were perplexed. They had agreed that Rob was indeed overworking, but to a large degree he was doing so because of the increasing expenses they saw looming on the horizon. His overtime was providing a nice nest egg for the kids' college costs, which would arrive before they knew it. They also wanted the kids to attend the same summer camps as their friends. There was also the issue of putting their youngest child in a better school. He was gifted, and they wanted to make sure he received the best education possible.

Sarah finally broke the silence. "Honey, I've been thinking that it may be time for me to get a job. That would be a great way to help fund some of these upcoming expenses, and it might allow you to cut back on the overtime. I don't see any other alternative. I really don't want the kids to miss out on summer camp, and I know their school activity fees are going to increase. By working outside the home I could help with those as well."

"I don't know," Rob said. "I'm not sure your income would accomplish what we'd hope."

Decision 2: Should Mom Work Outside the Home?

Rob and Sarah are face-to-face with the second important decision every couple needs to make. Should Sarah work outside the home? In many cases, couples may want Mom to stay home with the children, but when expenses increase as the family grows and matures, they begin to feel the squeeze financially.

I realize there are cases where a second income may be necessary to put food on the table, but my observation is that most times parents simply desire more for their children than the dad's income provides—more experiences, better schooling, or just more stuff. This seems to be the case with Rob and Sarah. Perhaps it's also the case with you.

As a couple, ask the same question Rob had the insight to ask: *Will a second income make that much difference?* Also, I want you to consider the real cost—financial and emotional—when a mother works outside the home. (For our discussion, "work" will be defined as "being gainfully employed in a vocation that takes the mother away from the home on a full-time basis.")

I watched a television special on latchkey kids. As they shared the story of an eight-year-old boy who had to lock himself in the house for three hours until his mother arrived home from work, I felt sad. This boy not only had to go straight home from school, but he couldn't turn on the microwave, talk to his friends, or go outside to play. He couldn't do anything except watch television until his mom came home. I didn't find it surprising that upon the mother's return, the child was reluctant to give her the hug and kiss she wanted.

Why have daycare centers popped up everywhere? Is it because both parents need to work to provide for the family? Or is it because today's culture defaults to the conclusion that both parents need to work? Beyond just the number of children in daycare, a survey titled "America After 3 PM" startled many experts with the finding that 14.3 million children, from kindergarten through twelfth grade, are in "self care," meaning home alone, after school.[1] Daycare centers often present many challenges to parents, including illnesses, overcrowding, and inadequate help, but the greatest tragedy is that people other than the parents are nurturing, teaching, and communicating values to millions of children.

I noted earlier that one of the God-given roles of a wife and mother is to nurture her children. Could the rise in childhood illnesses and personality problems be related to the lack of nurturing home environments during our children's formative years? After all, this is when children seek the comfort and love that home is supposed to provide.

I realize that this topic—and this decision—may be hard for many couples. Given their choice, many families would love to have Mom home with the children, but financially it just doesn't work. Or at least that appears to be the case. I'm going to encourage and challenge you to make sure that Mom's income is really necessary.

Reasons a Mother Works Outside the Home

The most common reason a mother works is the *need for additional income*—or at least a *perceived* need for additional income. An article in *The Atlanta Journal and Constitution* quoted several couples as saying they needed two incomes to make it. One mother commented, "I can't afford to stop working. It is not supplemental income anymore. I travel 110 miles a day, and I wouldn't do it if I didn't have to. If I didn't work, we wouldn't have clothes. We wouldn't have food."[2]

Though there are always exceptions, my observation from more than 30 years of counseling couples on finances is that only in rare cases does a mother work vocationally outside the home out of necessity. The reason this is true becomes clear as we analyze the actual contribution to the family's net income from a second salary. Let's consider for a moment what comes out of Mom's paycheck in the way of expenses, some of which are *fixed* while others are *variable*.

> *You should determine what actual expenses are...*
> *so you can correctly evaluate the true value of having*
> *Mom work outside the home.*

The two fixed (nondiscretionary expenses) are income taxes and tithing. (For this book, "tithe" is defined as 10 percent of gross income.) Income tax percentage is also fairly simple to calculate. Add up your total taxes (state, federal, social security) and divide the total by your gross income. This will give you an "effective" tax percentage so you will know what percentage of every dollar goes to taxes after deductions.

This tax percentage can be a pretty big range depending on what state you live in (some states have no taxes) and whether you are self-employed. Likely, this tax cost will be a minimum of 22 percent (employed in the lowest federal bracket with no state tax) but could be as high as 61 percent (self-employed with high state tax and top federal rate). A good estimate for most will be in the 30 percent range.

Given these assumptions, a best-case scenario would mean 60 percent of the income from Mom's job will be available for discretionary (additional) spending. And this only includes the fixed expenses.

Variable expenses associated with a second full-time job will differ from family to family. These expenses are less obvious than taxes and tithing, but they can take a big portion of a second salary. Meals, clothes, hairdresser, transportation costs, car repair and depreciation, daycare, and other miscellaneous costs, such as forfeited savings from not having time to shop sales, need to be factored in. I've found that when daycare costs, typically the greatest variable expense, is factored in, it generally takes $20,000 in annual salary before Mom is contributing to the family's discretionary funds.

You should determine what actual expenses are in each area so you can correctly evaluate the true value of having Mom work outside the home. Suffice it to say, the available amount will be significantly less than the gross salary, which may seem large and, at first glance, appear to be a big help to the family's finances.

I know in many cases variable expenses can be reduced by having family (often grandparents) care for the children, working from home, and other factors. However, the real question remains: "Is the additional income worth allowing somebody else to significantly participate in raising your posterity?"

My challenge to you is to make sure you've counted the financial, emotional, and long-term costs (James 4:13-15). Know exactly what the second income will be contributing to the total income before deciding whether Mom will develop a full-time career. Also make sure you clearly understand the concept of prosperity versus posterity (see chapter 1).

Another reason many women work outside the home is to get their emotional needs met. If the husband isn't encouraging his wife in her roles as homemaker and mother, it may be very easy for her to go into the marketplace to get positive reinforcement for her achievements. Work becomes the place she feels appreciated.

Men, if we don't encourage our wives, who will? After all, we love them and they're raising our most valuable possessions—our posterity. George Gilder, in his 1986 landmark book *Men and Marriage,* makes a telling point that is still true today:

> Women in the home are not performing some optional role that can be more efficiently fulfilled by the welfare state. Women in the home are not "wasting" their human resources. The role of the mother is the paramount support of civilized human society. It is essential to the socialization of men and of children. The maternal love and nurture of small children is an asset that can be replaced, if at all, only at vastly greater cost. Such attention is crucial to raising children into healthy productive citizens.[3]

The old adage "The hand that rocks the cradle rules the world" remains accurate. The following humorous story by an unknown author illustrates the importance of creating peace at home.

> A man came home from work and found his three children outside, still in their pajamas, playing in the mud, with empty food boxes and wrappers strewn all over the front yard. The door of his wife's car was open, as was the front door to the house. There was no sign of the dog.
>
> Proceeding into the entry, he found an even bigger mess. A lamp had been knocked over and the throw rug was wadded against one wall. In the front room, the TV was loudly blaring a cartoon channel, and the family room was strewn with toys and various items of clothing. In the kitchen, dishes filled the sink, breakfast food was spilled on the counter, the fridge door was open wide, dog food was spilled on the floor, a broken glass lay under the table, and a small pile of sand was spread by the back door.
>
> The man quickly headed up the stairs, stepping over toys and more piles of clothes, to look for his wife. He was worried she might be ill or that something terrible had happened. He was met with a small trickle of water as it made its way out the bathroom door. As he peered inside he found wet towels, scummy soap, and more toys strewn over the floor. Miles of toilet paper lay in a heap, and toothpaste had been smeared all over the mirror and walls.
>
> As he rushed to the bedroom, he found his wife curled up in bed wearing her pajamas and reading a novel. She looked up at him, smiled, and asked how his day went.

He looked at her with bewilderment and asked, "What happened here today?"

She smiled again and answered, "You know every day when you come home from work and ask me what in the world I did all day?"

"Yes," he replied.

"Well, today I didn't do it."

A third reason Mom might go to work outside the home is because of the slothfulness of her husband. The mother quoted in *The Atlanta Journal and Constitution* article was forced to drive 110 miles to work because her husband was lazy and not fulfilling his God-given responsibility of providing for the family (1 Timothy 5:8).

A husband who has slothful habits may gradually depend more and more on his wife as her career advances. My observation is that if the wife is content to live within the income the husband provides and is committed to him and encourages him, he will be motivated to provide what is needed. If not, there may be deeper marital issues that may require professional counseling.

I want to pause here and say that I recognize there are exceptions to what I'm writing. Not every family can be of the *Ozzie and Harriet* variety. But in our discussion of important financial decisions couples need to make, we're seeking *God's best* as it relates to His design for marriage and family. As we've discussed, that means the husband is the leader and provider and the wife is the helper, the nurturer, and the companion. I know this isn't politically correct, but being politically correct is often the enemy of truth.

A wife may go back to work to get some money of her own. If a husband is too tight with the cash and doesn't include his wife in spending decisions, his wife may decide she wants to work so she'll have money of her own. It's important for the harmony of the marriage that any budget or cash-flow system includes husband *and* wife having input in spending decisions.

A fifth reason for a wife to work is that the couple has materialistic expectations and aspirations. When other couples are living the good life, there's a natural desire to "keep up with the Joneses." Either spouse could have grown up in greater affluence than what the husband's salary now provides. If the income generated by the husband isn't enough to provide for the "finer" things (though the amount provided meets the family's needs), the couple may not be content. *Financial peer pressure is very real.* We get it from the media and even in Sunday school.

My advice for couples trying to live within what one income provides is to make friends with a few other couples who share the same family priorities and are spending and living accordingly. It's a lot cheaper and often as much fun to spend a day in a state park than it is to take a $5,000 ski vacation. Take simple steps to avoid financial temptation.

Finally, a woman may work because society has told her she can't be fulfilled as a person if she's "only" a homemaker. Everywhere she turns she's bombarded with the world's concept of working and told that working is the only way she can reach her potential and *be* somebody. After all, she's talented and went to college. She can't just throw all that training down the drain, can she? And why shouldn't she work in the marketplace? Hasn't the homemaker of yesteryear been replaced by the new career woman? Isn't the concept of superwoman valid? Can't a woman do it all—be a wife, mother, and have a career? (To gain more insight into this, sneak a peak at chapter 13, written by my wife, Julie.)

Women working vocationally outside the home is a difficult topic. The woman's primary roles, as we discussed briefly in chapter 2, are that of wife and mother. But what exactly does that mean? Is she confined to the home? What should she do with all her God-given talents? What should she do after she's fulfilled her responsibilities of being a full-time mother? What should she do after the children are grown or at least going to school? The guidelines found in Proverbs 31:10-31 are helpful:

An excellent wife, who can find? For her worth is far above jewels.

The heart of her husband trusts in her, and he will have no lack of gain. She does him good and not evil all the days of her life.

She looks for wool and flax, and works with her hands in delight. She is like merchant ships; she brings her food from afar. She rises also while it is still night, and gives food to her household, and portions to her maidens. She considers a field and buys it; from her earnings she plants a vineyard.

She girds herself with strength and makes her arms strong. She senses that her gain is good; her lamp does not go out at night. She stretches out her hands to the distaff, and her hands grasp the spindle. She extends her hand to the poor; and she stretches out her hands to the needy. She is not afraid of the snow for her household, for all her household are clothed with scarlet.

She makes coverings for herself; her clothing is fine linen and purple. Her husband is known in the gates, when he sits among the elders of the land. She makes linen garments and sells them, and supplies belts to the tradesmen.

Strength and dignity are her clothing, and she smiles at the future. She opens her mouth in wisdom, and the teaching of kindness is on her tongue. She looks well to the ways of her household, and does not eat the bread of idleness. Her children rise up and bless her; her husband also, and he praises her, saying: "Many daughters have done nobly, but you excel them all."

Charm is deceitful and beauty is vain, but a woman who fears the LORD, she shall be praised. Give her the product of her hands, and let her works praise her in the gates.

Proverbs 31 obviously describes a talented and gifted woman. We find a portrait of the wife of a man of rank. She is wise, careful, and godly in her domestic responsibilities within the home. She performs "marketplace vocational" functions ("she considers a field and buys it and plants a vineyard," verse 16). Note that she doesn't go into the marketplace to the exclusion of her home. All the functions she performs are done within the context of her "primary responsibility"—the home.

Scripture is clear in other places as well that a wife fulfills her role primarily by being in the home. "Your wife shall be like a fruitful vine within your house" (Psalm 128:3). The key guideline is that a woman should be involved in activities (vocational or volunteer) outside the home only if she is fulfilling her God-given roles within the home.

> *Just because a wife and mother can work*
> *outside the home, should she?*

In their book *Rocking the Roles,* Robert Lewis and William Hendricks write, "Unfortunately, the mistake many women are making today is in treating these core-role responsibilities as just options in a myriad of options. But a core role is not an option."[4] Some might argue that in Bible times society was agrarian, and as a result it was easier for a woman to be in the home and fulfill her role at the same time she was involved vocationally. Her vocation consisted of helping with the farm work. Others might suggest that labor-saving devices at home have given today's homemaker much more time, thus freeing her to work outside the home. Although a shift from an agrarian society to a highly automated, industrialized, urban society may make role fulfillment more difficult, the question remains the same. "Can a woman fulfill her God-given roles excellently and the way God intended and be involved outside the home, either in volunteer work or vocationally?" Just because a wife and mother *can* work outside the home, *should* she?

I know of many women who are doing excellent jobs fulfilling their God-given job descriptions and still have time to be involved in other activities. Many participate in volunteer work within their children's schools, neighborhood outreaches, discipling other women, political awareness activities, and other nonpaying jobs. Others take on jobs that either save them money or make money and yet allows schedule flexibility so they can be home when they need to be.

A wife and mother can also be involved vocationally and remain at home through home-based employment. An increasing number of corporations are hiring people with computers at home for telecommuting jobs, including data entry, claims processing, and word processing. Home-based workers also include accountants, architects, stockbrokers, computer programmers, and consultants. These vocations can be good alternatives for a family as long as the children remain the primary focus and are not considered a distraction.

Whether you have young school-age children or grown children, and whether you're employed in a paying vocation or involved in volunteer activities, everyone appreciates the awesome responsibility couples have in the development of their posterity.

And this isn't just a working mother issue. Stay-at-home moms can spend so much time volunteering, playing tennis, going to luncheons, helping at church, playing bridge, and being on community committees that they're not effectively fulfilling their roles at home. Likewise, husbands may spend too much time at work, on the golf course, watching TV, or in pursuit of other activities that take them away from their families. Parents must ask themselves whether they are spending their time in ways that reflect their desire to instill godly values and security in their children. If the answer is no, something needs to change.

Potential Consequences of Working Wives and Moms

One consequence of a working wife/mother is that she could usurp her husband's authority. This is especially true if she holds a responsible position or if she works for a strong, driven boss. As the wife becomes more independent, it's easy for her not to give honor and respect to her husband. This loss of God-given, male authority may cause tremendous resentment and stress in her husband. He may decide to look for someone else who respects him.

The more ambitious the wife is in her "outside the home" pursuits, the more stress she can put on the marriage. Although written many years ago, George Gilder's research on marriage is still insightful and applicable today:

American Couples, a work financed by the National Science Foundation and rated by the *New York Times* as the "largest and most comprehensive study ever undertaken on the subject of couples," concluded that "most men are not happy when their wives earn more than they do. When roles are reversed, with men doing the housework and women providing the income, couples become dreadfully unhappy. Women were found to be happier and relationships more stable when the male partners were ambitious and successful, but the husbands surveyed often resented ambitious wives."[5]

The 2009 edition of *The State of Our Unions: Marriage in America* noted: "Husbands are significantly less happy in their marriages, and more likely to contemplate divorce, when their wives take the lead in breadwinning."[6] Usurping her husband's authority can lead to another possible consequence—*role reversal.* I believe the greatest challenge facing couples today is to establish families according to biblical principles by getting the roles right and modeling them for the next generation.

We need families in which the husbands provide and the wives support, honor, and respect their husbands and nurture their children. If we think correctly about money and closely examine the myth of "we need two incomes to get by," we may find this goal achievable. If we don't model the correct roles, we run the risk of reaping the consequences in the next generation. We will have children growing up and marrying without having a clue about what the marriage relationship is all about. The moorings of the family will be loosened even more than they are at present. I first addressed this topic many years ago, and who would argue that the family is as solid today as it was just two decades ago?

One question wives sometimes ask at this point in our discussion is, "What if my husband isn't working hard?" I have two responses. First, make sure you're supporting and encouraging him in his role and communicating that you're willing to live within his income. Second, instead of taking things into your own hands, give him ample opportunity to provide. Remember that within each man is a God-given drive to provide. It is there! Wives, you can promote this drive or destroy it. The choice is yours.

Consider the example of Sweden, highlighted in Gilder's book *Men and Marriage*. Sweden has slowly destroyed the essential supports of the traditional nuclear family. Feminist pressure, among other factors, led to universal daycare, family planning programs, and paternity leaves for fathers. Tax laws were changed to favor two-income households and penalize maternal, stay-at-home care of preschool children. Families were penalized if children were not put into daycare. "The male role as principal provider was effectively abolished."[7]

The result in Sweden? "The marriage rate fell to the lowest level ever recorded in world demographic data. Forty percent of all births were illegitimate. The abortion rate soared. The economy foundered. Despite heavy taxes, the government deficit increased alarmingly."[8] Gilder warned that "the United States is enacting many of the policies that brought sexual suicide to Sweden." Even though we can observe what has happened in Sweden, we do not seem to be learning. Clearly, "profound and irretrievable damage [is] inflicted by a policy of driving mothers of small children out of the home and into the work force."[9] The effect is the same whether they are driven out by government intervention or by their own choices based on inaccurate data and ignorance of biblical truths.

The third consequence of wives and mothers working outside the home is they don't have the emotional and physical energy to fully invest in the next generation. Your children have needs, and most of their needs are unscheduled. Teachable moments can occur anytime. That's why children don't need just "quality time," they also need "all of the time." If Mom isn't present, she will miss many important times when her children need her. The myth about "quality time" over quantity time is a lie that has been propagated to excuse many people who are neglecting their children and spouses. It's difficult for either parent to be alert at home after a tough day at work because of the additional pressures and tensions, both physical and emotional, that the marketplace can produce. Also it's easy to transfer these pressures to the spouse and children.

More and more studies are showing how important it is to have a mother at home, especially with young children, for bonding, long-term security, and stability in their character, not to mention the inculcation of values. Dr. Willard Gaylin, psychiatrist and president of Hastings Center, a New York research center that studies ethical issues in medicine and the social sciences, has deep misgivings about substitute childcare. He believes children, especially infants, need a lot of nurturing and, although the mother is not the only one who can give the nurturing, she is the best one. He explains that in the first year, human contact is essential for the survival of the species. If a child is not taken care of psychologically as well as physiologically, his capacity for love, tenderness, affection, morality, and conscience can be destroyed by the way he is treated in those first few years.[10]

Robert Coles, noted research psychiatrist and Harvard Medical School professor, agrees. He says that because family life is such a low priority, lagging way behind self-indulgence and material gain, many children are experiencing an emotional deficit that is approaching tragic proportions. He's especially critical of the highly competitive, middle-income families. In the suburbs, there are children with their own kind of deprivation and disadvantage, where parents with six-figure incomes offer fancy homes, every kind of gadget, and trust funds—but no trust. Coles goes on to say, "A child's trust must be accumulated over the years, by constantly nurturing and attending to his emotional needs. Not 15 minutes of 'quality time'—but hours and hours and days and days of it."[11] All in all, every kid needs someone who is crazy about him or her and communicates that so the child knows.

And nothing could be more mistaken than the belief that a woman must work outside the home to contribute to the good of society. Gilder notes that...

> full-time work by mothers of small children comes at a serious twofold cost: first, the loss of the immeasurable social benefit of the mother's loving care for her child; second, the frequent loss of the husband's full-time concentration on his career. The yield of the mother's job to the economy or the man's help in the home only rarely can offset these costs of her employment. The society will pay the costs one way or another; not only through tremendous outlays for daycare but also through economic declines, population loss, juvenile delinquency, crime, mental illness, alcoholism, addiction, and divorce.[12]

Who can estimate the worth of a godly mother? Dr. Leila Denmark, a well-known Atlanta pediatrician who practiced into her 90s, made this statement:

> The hardest job on this earth, and the most important, is mothering. It's twenty-four hours for twenty-one years. When you take the baby out of the cradle and put it in a nursery (daycare), you've wrecked the nation. You can't tell them you love them and drop them off and drive off each day. One patient who was going back to work so they could buy a new house said, "Please check my baby for the nursery (daycare)." I said, "Do you mean to tell me you're selling that baby for a house? Twenty years from now that house will be no good and your baby will be gone."[13]

Parents, do we really want our posterity raised by somebody else while moms are pursuing more money?

Conclusion

Couples need to examine the financial myths of working mothers. As they weigh the decision whether or not Mom should work outside the home, couples need to look beyond finances and carefully weigh the consequences of not fulfilling their roles as husbands, wives, and parents.

If both parents working out of the home is the only option, perhaps due to the husband's job loss or illness, then my challenge to you is to prayerfully ask God to give you wisdom and creativity to structure your working situations to minimize the consequences on your family.

Game Plan

1. Do you and your spouse both work outside the home? If so, do you know the real contribution of the second income?

2. Why are you both working outside the home?

3. Could a reduction in expenses allow Mom to be at home? Will you consider doing that?

4. What is your greatest fear about living on the husband's income alone?

Chapter 7

The Checkbook

After processing the two work-related decisions: "How Much Should We Work?" and "Should Mom Work Outside the Home?", Rob and Sarah took a break to walk around the property at Village Crest. It was good to get outside and enjoy some fresh air. They felt like they had made great progress discussing some thorny financial issues, but they knew other issues had to be addressed. After their stroll, they were ready to discuss the third decision.

Decision 3: Who Pays the Bills?

When it comes to handling the family finances, one of two extremes can typically take place. One is where the husband controls the checkbook, asks for little or no input from his wife, and doles out any necessary money as the needs arise. The other is where the husband abdicates bill paying and lets his wife handle it. Both extremes can create anxiety and conflict in the relationship.

In this chapter we'll look at the reasons for both extremes, consequences to them, and actions you can take to promote marriage harmony when it comes to bill paying. Rob told Sarah early in their marriage that he knew more about money than she did; therefore, he could handle paying the bills better than she could. So Rob had always taken care of the bills. To be honest, I was really no different than Rob.

I'd always assumed I would handle the checkbook and pay the bills when I married. It never dawned on me as Julie and I drove away on our honeymoon that how we handled our money *together* was something that needed to be talked about.

The Dilemma of the Male Checkbook

Shortly after returning from our honeymoon, Julie and I had our first discussion about money. It started when I got ready to balance the checkbook and looked at Julie's ledger. She had written in most of the transactions, but there were a few missing—you know, check numbers written down with no dollar amounts beside them. I asked her about it, and she commented that she'd never really worried about tracking funds because she always knew there was enough money in her account.

That may have been okay when she was single, but now there were two of us using the same account, and I felt we needed to have more control. I had set up a nice budget with amounts for all the appropriate categories, and we needed to live within my carefully crafted plan. All I expected her to do was keep track of what she spent, and I would keep the running balance in my checkbook.

After getting the account balanced that month, I decided it would be wise if I knew more about what Julie was spending. Over the next few months, I asked her several times a day what she spent so I could keep the balance correct. Although my motive was pure, little did I realize that every time I asked her what she spent I was driving a small wedge into our relationship. She didn't feel I trusted her. We had to develop a better plan, and we did. (See chapter 8.)

Let's look at some reasons why a husband might exert excessive control over the family finances and ask for little input from his wife.

Reasons for the Control Dilemma

The first reason the husband might tightly control the purse strings is because he knows how tight the budget is and wants to keep a close rein on the funds so as not to blow the financial plan. In this scenario, the husband always asks his wife how much she's spent. Typical questions include: "Honey, did you write any checks today?" "What did you write checks for?" "How much cash do you have right now?" "Did you use much cash today?"

This was what I was doing. Julie and I had moved from Kansas, where we owned a house, to Atlanta, where we rented a place. I knew homes in Atlanta were 25 percent more costly than the ones in Kansas. Thus, I knew we really needed to watch our outflow to save additional funds for the down payment we would want to have for a house in Georgia. The problem was that I didn't discuss this with Julie.

In the scenario of the "male checkbook," the husband will not only ask questions about spending, but he will also find it very easy to become agitated if any of the money is spent in a way he doesn't think necessary. And when the purchases *are* necessary, he may question the amount spent. More than likely, he will think his wife spends too much. As he becomes more and more frustrated, he will resort to stricter control, which could result in going to the use of only one checkbook. If there is only one checkbook, he reasons, he has total control and she can't mess up the budget. He keeps the checkbook and ATM card and doles out cash as needed. In doing this, he has reduced the possibility of overspending by reducing her freedom—but he has also reduced his wife's flexibility and increased her frustration.

The second reason a husband may clamp down on finances is that his wife has done something with the finances that makes him uneasy. She may have spent money without his knowledge in a way that upset him. She may have spent money that caused an overdraft. She may have bought something he thought was frivolous or overpaid for it. Whatever happened, he has become more possessive of the funds, wants to keep very detailed records, and gives her less financial freedom.

The third reason a husband might exert excessive control over finances is his desire to keep his wife dependent on him. If he controls all the money and determines when, where, how, and how much is spent, he feels she will always need him. A man wants to have someone or something depend on him. He will provide, lead, and protect that someone or something. If his wife doesn't submit to him, follow his lead, and build him up as the provider and protector, he may wrongly try to use money to get her to respond the way he needs.

The Wife's Responses to the Husband's Excessive Control

The wife's first response may be apathy. Her thoughts on financial matters are negative because all she ever hears is "Why did you spend that?" "Why do you need more money for that?" "Isn't what I gave you enough?" "I can't believe you can't make it on what I give you." Since she feels she's fighting an uphill battle, she chooses to disengage. She had no input in the development of the budget and doesn't know why she is supposed to spend what he tells her. All she knows is that she has to continually report to him.

She tries to give her husband input about budget amounts, but he really isn't interested. He just wants her to stay within what he gives her with no questions asked. So she decides not to care because it's easier than getting upset about the situation.

The clueless husband doesn't understand why she doesn't get with the program. He wonders why she isn't enthusiastic about the budget. Since she doesn't seem to care, he gets more frustrated and exerts more control. And the vicious cycle continues.

A second reaction to the husband's extreme financial control is the wife may spend frivolously. Her motivation could be revenge, apathy, or just a lack of spending goals. Whatever may be the case, the wife won't take responsibility for her spending. Since she's not part of the budgeting process and her husband won't talk to her about it, overspending is a good way to get his attention. She thinks that if she is always short on money, it might get his attention. Then he may listen to her and explain what is going on with their finances.

Yes, overspending may indeed get his attention if he is tuned in to her. More often than not, however, it just adds fuel to the fire. His distrust about her spending increases. As the trust level falls, he restricts her freedom even more. And the overall frustration and anxiety level in the marriage rises higher.

A third response to excessive financial control by the husband is that his wife may hide money. Since talking to her husband about money and asking him for money upsets him, she decides to hide some of it in case she needs it later. Any budgeted money she doesn't spend is secretly socked away. The wife feels the only way to have the money she needs is to be deceptive. She may eventually use that extra money without telling him and, perhaps, in ways which he might disagree.

I recently sat down with a couple to help them with their finances. I guess the wife felt it was a safe place because the first thing she said was, "I've been hiding money from him in order to do some of the things I want to do." Wow, what a way to begin a meeting! The interesting thing was the husband's response. He said, "I knew all along." Secretiveness isn't a solid foundation on which to build a harmonious marriage. Strong marriages are built on truthfulness and transparency, not deception and dishonesty. This couple was going to face some serious challenges if they didn't change their communication patterns regarding money.

Many times a wife may want a nest egg to be able to buy something special for her husband. This is a legitimate desire. If she doesn't work outside the home or have the ability to generate funds of her own, so to speak, then the budget system needs to be designed to allow her to have some discretionary funds. This will take away the temptation to hide money or lie to get extra money for the gift. If she must ask her husband for money and account for every penny, that takes the fun out of buying him a present.

Another way a wife might respond to being restricted financially is to want to get a job (or keep a job she already has) so she can have her own money. Since she doesn't have a say in the family money, she will go to work and earn her own.

There's no greater way to disrupt harmony and promote disunity in a marriage than to have "his" money and "her" money. When a man and a woman marry, they become one. This includes financial oneness.

It's not uncommon to counsel a couple and hear them say they have two separate accounts. When I ask them why, there's usually a long pause. The answer is something to the effect that they feel it's easier this way. I interpret having separate accounts as their way of avoiding the communication that should and must take place for maximum harmony in the marriage. I've never seen separate accounts solve any budget problems. As a matter of fact, it usually compounds the bookkeeping problems and contributes to overspending.

Another negative aspect of having separate accounts is that it promotes a lack of trust. Working from the same account is a great way to build trust and develop harmony. In today's culture, it's not uncommon for a couple planning marriage to negotiate and sign a prenuptial agreement. This agreement says in effect, "Just in case things don't work out, I want to make sure I keep all of my assets." Wow! What a sad way to start a marriage. Each party is saying up front, "I don't really trust you. I really don't want you to have a part of what is mine. Let's keep some things separate." With that kind of a start, there will most certainly be problems.

Solving the Excessive Control Dilemma

Conflict over finances can be avoided by implementing two important principles:

- Work together to determine budget category amounts
- Have a cash flow plan

The first thing a husband must do to solve the dilemma of excessive financial control is to include his wife in the process of *developing* the budget. Instead of creating a budget the wife must fit into, the result of joint planning will truly create a budget that belongs to both of them. They will each feel an element of responsibility to make sure the budget plan is carried out. The goal of making the budget work is held by both parties. Instead of working against each other, they are on the same team.

Julie and I sit down at the end of the year to discuss our budget. I share with her our overall financial plan for the upcoming year. We look at income, taxes, and charitable giving. We review our prior year expenditures. I then get her input on budget items, such as groceries, clothing, medical costs, and so on. I'm especially attentive to her input on the items she's responsible for and in a far better position to know realistic amounts than I am, such as grocery costs. We then set the budget for the coming year.

If the wife is involved in the process of determining the budget, not only will the husband get more accurate amounts, but he will attain much greater motivation on the part of his wife to make the system work. In our situation, one of the reasons Julie was frustrated was because she didn't know *why* we were on the budget I'd designed. Once we discussed how much we needed to purchase a house in Georgia, she was more than happy to do her part to make the system work.

Involve your wife in the process of managing the family finances. Here's a great example when thinking about budgeting together. Think about doubles tennis for a minute. What if only one partner—the husband—had a racket? Can you imagine how helpless the partner with no racket must feel? That is how the wife feels if she doesn't have an active part to play in establishing the family spending plan. (And vice versa, if the wife handles the finances without including the husband.)

> *Husbands, part of our responsibility is to involve our wives in the budgeting process so they will be aware of what is going on financially in case something happens to us.*

Involving the wife in handling the finances has the benefit of also encouraging her skills in handling money if something happens to the husband. In my business, it's not uncommon to run across widows whose husbands handled all the financial issues with no involvement on her part. In these cases, the recent widows didn't have a clue about how to pay the bills, what bills there were to pay, and when to pay them. They also didn't know where the wills were, what insurance policies were in force, and even how many bank accounts they had or where they were.

Husbands, part of our responsibility is to involve our wives in the budgeting process so they will be aware of what's going on financially in case something happens to us. It's also important to establish good relationships with people you trust so your wife can turn to them for advice in case of your death. I've found that this is one of the reasons many of our clients have established a working relationship with our firm. By already having a relationship established with us, the husband gives the wife a place to turn for trusted financial and estate counsel if something happens to him.

Although I balance our family checkbook, I periodically ask Julie to do it so she knows what's going on. It helps her know what bills we have, how much they are, and when they're due. We also go over our wills, insurance, and investments once a year to make sure we're on the same page.

The wife should have a checkbook, debit card, credit card, and cash, just as the husband does. She shouldn't be relegated to "being on the dole" for cash. She should have the same cash-flow resources as the husband. If discord arises, both husband and wife should ask themselves hard questions. As head of the household, the husband should lead in this. He should first examine his motives. Why does he want to handle the finances this way? Is he being over-controlling? Why does he want to have so much control? Has lack of communication contributed to unhealthy practices, such as excessive control, deception, or hoarding cash? The wife should examine her motives to see if she's doing all she can to respect and honor her husband and work with him to steward their finances in a God-honoring way. A godly couple should strive to make Psalm 34:3 a verse for their relationship: "O magnify the LORD with me, and let us exalt His name together."

Does He Even Care?

As Rob and Sarah continued their discussion regarding how they handled the finances, Rob acknowledged that he probably was too controlling with the checkbook. He felt that he was justified in his actions. He'd watched his mother struggle to manage his parents' finances, and he never wanted that burden to be on Sarah. He admitted the pendulum had probably swung too far, but his father had been aloof when it came to finances, removed from everyday spending decisions. He never seemed to know what was going on with the family's money, nor did he seem to care. Rob also recalled that the problem seemed compounded by his father's excessive use of credit cards and random cash withdrawals. Far too many times Rob heard his mother's frustrated comments when she was paying the bills and balancing the bank statement.

Sarah appreciated Rob sharing his background in this area because it helped her understand why he'd kept such tight control over the checkbook. It didn't take away the hurt she'd experienced because of it, but at least she better understood why Rob operated the way he did. She couldn't help but wonder why Rob's dad was so apathetic.

I'll never forget the night Julie and I were asked to meet with a young couple who said they were having trouble in their marriage due to finances. As we listened to them, the first insight that became obvious was that the husband wasn't involved at all in the finances. In fact, the extent of his participation in the budget process was to use his ATM card to get cash whenever he needed it. It was up to his wife to keep the checkbook updated and balanced even though she wasn't always aware of his withdrawals until the bank statement arrived. This approach caused her to become resentful and angry. She knew the budget was tight, but when she tried to talk to him and get his input, he wasn't interested.

Why does this happen? Why would a husband not care about the family finances? Why would he choose to leave bill paying and budgeting entirely up to his wife?

Reasons for Husband Apathy Regarding Finances

One reason a husband may abdicate the bill-paying responsibility is that he separates his personal financial responsibilities from his work responsibilities. He may figure he's working long, hard hours to make the money, so once it's in the bank his wife can deal with it. He has plenty to think about in providing for his family without being bothered with small issues, such as which bills should be paid and when; what amounts should be spent on gifts, groceries, kids clothes, school supplies; and what should be allotted to savings. He may also conclude he really doesn't have time to pay the bills, and that function is the least his wife can do to help since he's providing the income.

He might conclude that he needs to spend time building his skills to be better at his job instead of handling the family budget. He feels the money seems sufficient for their lifestyle, and his wife can do whatever she wants with the money as long as she doesn't overspend.

Another reason a husband may refuse to be involved in the budgeting process is that he feels like a failure. If cash flow is tight and barely enough to cover living expenses, each time he has to make a decision about what bills to pay and not pay, he's reminded the income is inadequate, which he interprets as his failure to provide. As a result, he withdraws from the process. It's easier to ignore the problem than face his perceived short-comings as a husband and provider.

Along with a feeling of failure, the husband may fear accountability. He reasons that if he doesn't have to deal with the budget, he can escape the reality of the responsibility. I've observed that this lack of account-ability usually manifests itself in the misuse of credit cards and cash cards. I've met with couples where the husband was continually getting cash at the ATM machine or charging items and letting the wife worry about how to get the budget and checkbook to balance.

> *The husband's responsibility is to make sure there's enough income to meet the family's budgeted needs.*

In the myriad of financial plans I've helped couples develop over the years, it's been the exception when the wife is the one to blow the bud-get. In most cases, if there is a living-expense problem it's the use of the credit cards and excessive cash withdrawals by the husband that are the culprits. This makes sense because, as we learned earlier, the wife usually wants security, and her security would feel threatened if she overspent.

A third reason a husband may be removed from the budgeting process is that his temperament is such that he doesn't like dealing with numbers and details. As a result, he transfers the responsibilities to pay the bills and balance the checkbook to his wife. As I've worked with couples, I've found that many times the entrepreneurial, gregarious, outgoing man may find it difficult to get involved with his family's finances. His per-sonality tends to be much more relational and less detailed, making it easier for him to transfer financial responsibilities to his wife. In some cases this isn't a bad thing, especially if the wife likes numbers and has an aptitude for them. However, if she doesn't have these skills or the desire, financial anxiety and stress can wear on the marriage relationship.

As we will see in the next chapter, who handles the day-to-day bill paying isn't that important. What does matter is that the husband is shouldering the burden of responsibility for the living expenses. The husband's responsibility is to make sure there's enough income to meet the family's budgeted needs. He shouldn't leave his wife in the role of having to decide what bills to pay and what ones not to pay when there isn't enough income. His temperament isn't an excuse for abdicating his provision responsibility.

The Wife's Response to the Husband's Financial Apathy

If the husband isn't involved at all in the budgeting process, *the wife's response usually includes agitation, frustration, and fear—especially if funds are tight.* She's upset with him for putting her in the uncomfortable position of trying to make the income stretch to pay all the bills with no input from him. She worries about which bills to pay and which ones not to pay each month. She's upset and afraid when creditors call and overdraft notices from the bank come in the mail. Men, it's embarrassing for our wives to cover for us, so we need to be careful not to put them in that situation.

Next, the wife's security may be threatened by the husband's apathy. Paying bills can make the wife more acutely aware of how much money it takes to meet the family's needs. On one hand, this is good because it helps her understand the cost of running the household, and it helps prepare her to carry on if something happens to the husband. On the other hand, if the husband isn't involved with helping prioritize the use of limited funds, it can threaten her security, resulting in her worrying more. She may question if her husband is caring for her adequately.

Interestingly, husbands may conclude that their wives will only get frustrated if funds are tight. To the contrary, wives can also be frustrated if there are unlimited funds and the husband still provides no input. With an unlimited budget she's insecure because there are no boundaries. If she spends too much, will he become angry and frustrated with her? No input or communication from the husband may make her insecure no matter how much or how little money exists.

> *Money can either be a promoter or destroyer of communication.*

In a recent meeting with a couple, the wife said, "I just want to know what I'm responsible for and where the boundaries are. I don't like not knowing what's expected of me." Her husband generated a six-figure income, and they spent $10,000 per month on living expenses. Most wives don't want to set the boundaries. They want their husbands involved. Wives want to know the boundaries exist and where. This gives them much more security.

A third response a wife may have to her husband's apathy is the desire to become independent. Since she has the responsibility for handling the finances, she makes more and more money decisions without consulting her husband. This could lead to less communication and a tendency to drift apart. He doesn't want to be bothered and likes to be left alone so she quits talking to him. Money can either be a promoter or destroyer of communication. In the case of apathy, it gradually becomes a destroyer.

Finally, the wife may lose respect for her husband. Since he's not giving her the leadership and direction she desires in the financial area, she gradually loses respect for his position. Although her role is to honor and respect her husband, it's tough for her to do because she feels alone in the money arena. As her respect dwindles, she may find it easier to belittle him and tear him down. She finds it much more difficult to build him up and give him the encouragement he needs.

Isn't it amazing what a temporal, nonessential, functional medium of exchange (money) can do to a marriage? What the husband craves—respect, encouragement, and honor—isn't present because he abdicated his role of leadership in the money area. And much of it is because he's reticent to contribute to the conversation about the budget and make sure his wife isn't stressed about it. What are some solutions to the problem of husband apathy?

Solution to a Husband's Apathy

The first part of the solution is for the husband to understand and embrace his role as provider. First Timothy 5:8 says, "If anyone does not provide for his own, and especially for those of his household, he has denied the faith and is worse than an unbeliever." This provision is not only "bringing home the bacon" but also having input into how the bacon is used.

Men, whether we make much or little, we are accountable before

God for how the funds are used. As a husband, even if your wife has an aptitude for numbers and likes to handle them, you are responsible for the overall direction and providing input regarding your family's finances. Our wives are our helpers in the process, but they are not the ones God will ask, "How did you do with what I entrusted to you?" He will ask us men. (Husbands, if you don't think this is your responsibility, reflect on God's questioning in the Garden of Eden. God came to the couple, but He "called to the man" (Genesis 3:9). Adam, not Eve, was responsible for the family unit, and as a result God asked Adam how they—not just Adam but both of them—did regarding the directions He'd given them.) How will you answer for your responsibility for the money God entrusted to you?

The second part of the solution is to determine who will keep the books. Who will have the overall responsibility for balancing the checkbook and paying the bills? The husband may delegate all or part of the bookkeeping to his wife. She may like working with numbers and have desires and abilities in this area. He may be too busy to give it appropriate care. If he delegates this task to his wife, he needs to make sure he retains responsibility for priority decisions, especially when funds get tight. He also needs to be sure that he delegates only as much of this responsibility as his wife feels comfortable handling or desires to handle.

Julie and I have "assigned accountability." We each are responsible for paying certain bills. We also feel it's best if I balance the checkbook monthly because it maintains my focus and constantly sharpens my awareness of my responsibility before the Lord. (Besides that, Julie hates to do it.)

A third part of the solution is to realize that a money surplus does not negate the need for guidelines and communication. As we learned, a wife's security is enhanced with boundaries. So even if a couple has way more income than is needed for basic living expenses, they should still take time to talk through financial issues and details. This will increase their ability to be good stewards of what God entrusts to them.

The final part of the solution is for the wife to encourage her husband. One of the reasons for his lack of interest may be that he feels like a failure because he thinks he's not being a good provider by making enough money. A wife can spur her husband on to embrace his provider responsibility by letting him know she's committed to living within his income and, beyond that, she is on his team. Julie did a great job of this with me right after we married. She said, "I would live in a tent in Alaska with you." What this meant to me was that she would be content with whatever I made and live wherever we could afford. (I knew she really meant it because Julie doesn't like to be cold.) It's much more difficult for the husband to be apathetic when he knows his wife is for him and is his greatest cheerleader.

Conclusion

I encourage you to put this book down for a minute and make a commitment to God and to your spouse that you will no longer allow bill paying to be a problem in your marriage. Make a commitment to do whatever needs to be done to reduce the potential volatility that can result without a mutually agreed upon spending plan. Develop a system that will work for you and your spouse to promote harmony and unified trust in your marriage. (The next chapter offers some ideas for doing this.) Make a commitment to better fulfill the roles that God has assigned to you, whether it is "headship" or "helper." Make Philippians 2:2-4 true as it relates to finances and your marriage:

> Make my joy complete by being of the same mind, maintaining the same love, united in spirit, intent on one purpose. Do nothing from selfishness or empty conceit, but with humility of mind regard one another as more important than yourselves; do not merely look out for your own personal interests, but also for the interests of others.

Game Plan

1. Is bill paying a source of conflict in your marriage? Why or why not?

2. How have your temperaments impacted the decision of who pays the bills and handles the checkbook?

3. Did your family backgrounds influence how you've decided to pay the bills in your house?

4. How do you set boundaries regarding spending?

5. How much time do you spend discussing spending issues?

6. Do you spend too much time, just the right amount of time, or not enough time communicating on finances? Explain.

Chapter 8

Freedom in Control

Rob and Sarah were glad it was time for lunch. Though they'd made good progress, the discussion on bill paying and handling the checkbook had left them both a little frustrated. Sarah felt she better understood why Rob was so controlling. She was sure she didn't want to handle the entire checkbook process herself, so she was hoping they'd discover a better way. Surely they could make this area less stressful in their marriage. Their next decision would go a long way in determining if that would be the case.

Decision 4: How Do We Set Budget Amounts?

"Hey, honey, this is interesting," Sarah said, breaking the silence.

"What's that?"

"This CD in the packet is by the same guy who spoke on budgeting at my friend Meg's Sunday school class."

"What's his name?"

"Russ...Russ Crosson. Meg said his advice was very helpful."

"I don't know," Rob said tiredly. "There doesn't seem to be a simple way to budget."

"What would it hurt to hear it?" Sarah asked. "We could listen to it over lunch. And if it's not good, we'll just turn it off and try to figure out a budget process on our own."

"I suppose we could give it a try," Rob said. "I'm sure I saw a CD player on a shelf in the living room."

Fifteen minutes later Sarah put the CD in the player, and she and Rob listened to the message offered in the rest of this chapter.

Why Budget?

Hi, I'm Russ Crosson, and thanks for being here today to hear about the dreaded "B" word. My wife, Julie, never liked the word "budget," so we call it "planned spending." Whatever you call it, each couple must determine how they're going to budget and control their spending. As we begin, please understand there are two basic reasons to budget.

First, budgeting allows you freedom in your finances. Freedom is having guidelines and boundaries that, when adhered to, help you live within your income. Budgeting makes it less likely you'll succumb to the lure and pressures of the world—the lust of the eyes and the lust of the flesh, which is referred to in 1 John 2:15-16. You're better able to resist the temptation to overspend because you know what you have available to spend, why you're spending it, where you are on the spending plan, and the long-term rewards of sticking with it. The boundaries a budget provides, rather than being restrictive, give a sense of security.

Second, budgeting makes money a nonissue in marriage. Julie and I experienced some friction regarding money early on in our marriage. By learning how to develop a budget and, together, implementing a system to stay on budget, we've eliminated money as a problem or stress between us. If both of you will work together to implement the steps that follow, you can take something that's potentially divisive and make it a source of harmony and teamwork.

The Budget in Context

For the purpose of this discussion, I will define budget as "what is planned to be spent on living expenses." Before couples can develop a "living expense budget," they must first take these steps:

- Step 1: Agree as a couple on the annual *charitable giving* amount

- Step 2: Prepare an *income tax projection* and set tax withholdings accordingly
- Step 3: Determine the *minimum annual debt repayment* amount

After these three steps are taken and subtracted from your total income, you will have a number that will be the *maximum available* for your family's living expenses.

As you discover how to establish a budget, refer to the "Living Expenses Worksheet" at the end of this book for a visual sample.

Keys to Building Your Budget

Don't leave necessary categories unbudgeted. In more than 30 years of working with folks, one of the most common mistakes made when setting a budget is to leave out important categories. For instance, it's not uncommon to leave out expenses when you don't know in advance what the costs will be, such as auto repairs, home repairs, medical expenses not covered by insurance, and kids' activity fees.

I received a letter from a gentleman that drove home this point: "I have never really gripped the cost of day-to-day living. I sweep things like clothes, gasoline, dental expenses, brakes, and gifts into a little pile called incidentals. Well, it's not a little pile called incidentals, it's a big pile called essentials. Not only was the pile larger, the category was wrong." This guy was always spending more than he made because he didn't have a good grasp on what he had to earn to cover his living expenses. If you don't budget for everything, you may think you're earning enough to live at your present level, but all the while you're really fooling yourself.

> *Don't forget that anything being withheld from your paycheck should be included as part of your budget.*

My encouragement to you is to look at prior years' records to determine *all* the outlays for which you need to plan. Between this information and the Living Expense Worksheet at the end of this book, you should have a good framework to ensure you don't leave anything out when creating your budget.

Once you have all the appropriate categories budgeted, make sure it doesn't total more than the maximum amount available (income - charitable giving - taxes = monies available for expenses). If the living expenses exceed that amount, you will need to cut back someplace or generate more income.

One more important point. Don't forget that anything being withheld from your paycheck should be included as part of your budget. Many times people forget to include expenses such as medical insurance payments and 401(k) deposits. Just because they're withheld and you aren't writing checks for them doesn't mean they shouldn't be part of your budget. After all, you *are* spending money for them.

Be realistic on your budget amounts. A second common mistake couples make is to be unrealistic on the budget amounts to make the living expense numbers fit within the maximum available amount available to spend. They think if they put in a lower amount to make sure all the categories are covered, somehow it will work out. But if you do this, not only will you not be able to stay on the budget, but when you exceed the budget amounts, you will typically go into debt to cover the shortfall. This was the case with the gentleman I just mentioned who lumped many of his expenses together.

Setting realistic amounts is where both husband and wife need to weigh in. Who is likely to know the best grocery amount for the family or a reasonable amount to set aside for the kids' clothes? Husband or wife? I remember when I set our first budget and told Julie she had $150 a month to spend for groceries. What a joke that turned out to be! After a few days of eating beans, I decided it was better to consult her so we could set a more realistic grocery amount. Including her in setting budget amounts has resulted in much more harmony. Not only does she help set several of the amounts, but she's part of the process so she has a vested interest in keeping to the budget. By both being involved in the process, it's much easier than if I had set the budget in a vacuum.

Give your budget time to work (12 to 18 months). Many couples give up on a budget too soon. They exceed the budgeted amount in a category or an emergency comes up, so they conclude it's not possible to stay on a budget. When Julie and I began our spending plan, we came to realize we really didn't know what amounts we should budget for gifts, clothes, utilities, and so on. It took the better part of two years to determine realistic amounts and adapt our spending habits to fit within our budget.

Keys to a System that Works

Once you have a budget set, it's time to develop a system to ensure you stay within the budget. This is where many couples fail. One reason is because they think they're on a budget when they're really following a record-keeping system. What do I mean by that? Occasionally, when I've asked couples if they're on a budget, they reply, "Yes, we use Quicken."

It's fine that they use Quicken, but that's not a budget system. Quicken is a record-keeping product. It may allow you to set your budget amounts more realistically, but it doesn't help you stay within your budget.

You're only on a budget system if, at any point in time, you can answer this question: *How much do you have left to spend on [name a specific expense].* It's not enough to be able to determine what you've spent; you need to be able to quickly know how much you have *left to spend* for the year so you can stay within the budgeted amount. Julie and I have found the following concepts and ideas common to systems that work.

Any system is in essence an "envelope system."[1] What this means is that you have put your "budgeted amount" into an envelope, and then you spend out of it for the specific expense until it's gone. Obviously you're not likely to put large amounts of cash for your mortgage, utilities, gifts, car insurance, and vacation in literal envelopes, but essentially the system you use will work the same way.

Let me illustrate. Assume the amount budgeted for auto repair for the year is $2,000. Your car breaks down in March and costs $750 to repair. You pay the bill, and you have $1,250 left in the envelope, so to speak. You are still on budget. Or what if you budget $500 per month for utilities, but during an unusually cold winter month you spend $600? You're over budget that one month, but you won't know if you're over or under the complete amount in your budget for this item until the end of the year. The spring and summer months may not require as much electricity or water, so you find you're right on budget.

I can guess what you're thinking. "Russ, how can I do that? Spend $600 when I only budgeted $500?" This is where the second key principle comes in.

No system will work without cash on hand. If you're trying to stay on budget and live paycheck to paycheck, it will blow up on you. Why? Because expenses aren't linear. They don't necessarily occur in the exact month you need them to. The great clothing sale at the mall may fall at the same time one of the kids gets sick, the car breaks down, and it's the coldest month on record so your utility bill spikes. I've never seen a couple be able to stay on a budget system if they're living paycheck to paycheck. See the "Common Budget Questions Answered" after the conclusion in this chapter for suggestions for what to do if you're in this situation.

I recommend having an emergency fund of three- to six-months living expenses in reserve, not only for emergencies, but also to prime the "living expenses" pump. At least one month's reserve will allow you to start a budget system. By having cash in the system, you can handle the utilities being slightly higher in January; you'll be able to pay for the car repair in February even if you have a trip with your wife planned for Valentine's Day, all the while staying on your overall annual budget. (In a later chapter we'll discuss more about having money in reserve.)

Differentiate between **monthly** *items and* **non-monthly** *items.* Once you've completed the Living Expense Worksheet, go back through and determine which are non-monthly expenses. There could be others, but for most couples the big six are auto repair (and insurance), home repair and maintenance, medical (the co-pay, not the monthly insurance amount), gifts, vacation, and clothes.

Separating out what is monthly and what isn't is often a breakthrough for most couples when budgeting. Why? Because they understand for the first time *why* their budget system wasn't working. They were trying to budget for annual expenses on a monthly basis and that doesn't work. Budgets need to be annual, not monthly. You will *fund* your budget monthly, but you should plan for expenditures on an annual basis. Let me illustrate.

Let's say we allocate $2,000 for each of the six non-monthly budget items (auto, home upkeep, medical co-pays, gifts, vacation, clothes). That comes to $167 a month. But is that how the bills usually end up coming? No. These expenses happen unexpectedly or when you plan them (a vacation or gifts, for example). Your car doesn't break down at $167 per month, and you don't buy clothes at $167 per month. The kids don't get gifts or need medicine at $167 per month. So you need cash *in the system* to prime the annual pump. And you can refill "the cash" with the monthly funding.

Here is how it should work. Let's say you have cash set aside ("in the system") at the beginning of the year. Your car needs a $300 repair in January, you find a great clothing sale where you spend $500, and you take a little getaway with your spouse for $200. You can do all that and not blow your budget. Why? Remember, I said earlier that any budget must answer the question: How much do I have left? Since we allocated $2,000 per expense category, you have $1,700 left in auto repair, $1,500 in clothing, and $1,800 in vacation. You're still on budget even though you spent $1,000 while only putting $500 ($167 per month x 3) in the annual fund during January.

> *Never use credit cards for monthly items.*

Obviously you can't overspend every month and have your budget survive, but I'm sure you get the idea. By the way, I've found that by making this designation of non-monthly expenses, folks can stretch their vacation, clothes, and gift dollars by taking advantage of sales and deals. A month-to-month or paycheck-to-paycheck system doesn't allow for that.

Another reason this distinction is important is that typically it's the non-monthly expenses that blow most budgets; therefore, controlling them will go a long way to ensuring you stay on track. Typically utilities are in a pretty tight band; the mortgage is what it is; and gas for the car, groceries, eating out, and kids lunches are usually very close to the same each month.

I'm not saying people can't overspend in a monthly category. It's just that typically any overspending on monthly expenses is minor when considering the big picture. Julie and I have found in counseling couples that grasping this distinction is the biggest key to having a cash-flow system that works.

Never use credit cards for monthly items—use cash, checks, or a debit card. The only way you'll know if you're on budget with your monthly expenses is if you pay them monthly. Remember the envelope method? If you don't pay for an expense monthly, how can you answer the question about how you are doing?

I've been confronted many times on the recommendation to not use credit cards for monthly expenses. A couple will challenge me with the idea that a person gives up earning "redeemable points" if they don't use their credit card. Or they ask me about the danger of using debit cards. I understand these issues, but I contend that being current month-to-month to ensure we're on budget is more important in the long run. I do allow for credit card use for non-monthly, annual expenses, especially online purchases, such as clothes, in case they need returned, and other such items.

Any system you decide to use must not be too complicated. Most systems that fail are too complicated to be sustainable. Although it seems like a good idea to keep track of every dime spent on Cokes, a latte, nail polish, or a sleeve of golf balls, if that's your long-term plan, it will probably die. Yes, you may want to write everything down at first to establish realistic expense amounts, but don't plan to do that long term. Julie and I have found that if we set realistic budget amounts, we only need to go back and get into the details if we find we've overspent in a category. And since we're aware of how much is left each month or year, we can usually adjust our spending accordingly and not have to track every detail.

Assign responsibility. Review the Living Expense Worksheet at the end of this book and decide who will be responsible for what expenses. Even though the husband has the overall responsibility to make sure there's enough income, it's practical to assign each expense item to the spouse who is most likely to deal with that expense. For example, it's easier for Julie to buy the groceries than me, so keeping track of grocery money is also easier for her. It's also more prudent for her to handle medical expenses, clothing, and incidental costs. On the other hand, we both need an allocation for gasoline and miscellaneous cash. I pay the utilities and various insurances.

As I noted earlier, it doesn't matter which spouse pays the bills as long as the husband understands that in his role of provider he needs to make sure the income is sufficient to meet the living expenses. And as long as both spouses have equal input into the budget amounts and there is agreement on who is paying what, you should be in harmony on finances.

I've seen many cases where the wife is more detailed than the husband, and she likes to pay all the bills. The husband basically gets an allowance for miscellaneous items, such as lunches and gasoline. On the other hand, I've seen cases where the husband pays most all the bills except for a few his wife is responsible for. It really doesn't matter as long as the system promotes harmony and communication.

Use one account—no "his" and "hers." When you got married, you chose to become one and to dwell together in harmony. Your finances are no longer each of yours but *both* of yours. Even if you choose to use multiple accounts for your system of control, remember that the money (in total) belongs to both of you. Julie and I have found that having one account from which we both pay bills works best. This way if she spends something for me (gas for my car) or I pick up groceries on my way home (which she is responsible for), we can simply make a journal entry to transfer funds to the appropriate person. We don't have to physically move money from one person to the other. We simply move from "one envelope to another."

Conclusion

I hope you've enjoyed this overview of budgeting and have heard some ideas that might be helpful in developing a system to promote harmony in the financial area of your marriage. Thank you for listening!

"That was interesting!" Rob exclaimed. "Much better than I expected. I think there might be some things we heard that we can implement to make our bill paying and checkbook management less stressful."

"I agree," Sarah chimed in.

"We can make copies of the Living Expense Worksheet for a starting point. Before we get down and dirty on the details, what do you say we get some more fresh air? I could use an invigorating break. That 'meal' on finances was more than I bargained for," Rob said with a yawn.

"I couldn't agree more!" Sarah said. "Let's go!"

Common Budget Questions Answered

Can we start using a budget system anytime during the year?

Yes, although it's easiest to start at the beginning of a calendar year, you can start anytime. You need to go through the same process to determine the calendar year amounts. You then allocate the monthly amounts just like we discussed. On the annual amounts, you will deduct what you've already spent to that point in the year, and you will prorate the remaining amounts throughout the rest of the year.

What if I don't have a set salary because I work on commission or do freelance work?

If you have a variable income, you can begin by putting more into your savings. You can then deposit your variable checks into your savings account and, in essence, salary yourself out of the savings account each month. In other words, you put yourself on a set salary each month, thus removing the monthly variability. You still have to earn a certain level to cover your expenses (living, giving, taxes, debt payments), but "paying yourself a salary" should make budgeting easier.

Evening out your monthly cash flow for budgeting purposes removes potential marriage stressors that affect couples with variable incomes.

Note: Even if you're on a salary, you may want to deposit paychecks into a savings account and pay yourself each month versus trying to figure what to pay from the paycheck on the first and the fifteenth. In other words, go to a one-time-a-month allocation to fund living expenses instead of two times a month.

Do we have to have only one checking account?

No. You need to adapt the system you choose to fit you and your spouse. Julie and I have found that one account makes for more flexibility and less paperwork. You may find that you like to allocate to separate accounts. You may have a relationship with more than one bank and, as a result, want to have more than one account. You can have as many accounts as you want. Just remember that the more accounts you have, the more "minimum balances" you need to maintain. Also be sure to avoid the problem of "his" and "her" money, as discussed in chapter 7.

What if we don't have cash saved to "prime the expenses pump"?

You need to do whatever is necessary to come up with some savings. It's impossible to make any budget system work without a cash cushion. You may need to sell an asset, work a second job for a period of time, or sacrifice in some area until you have accumulated enough to make the system you choose work. Having at least one month of expenses is enough to get started.

What if I have items deducted from my paycheck, such as insurance premiums?

Make sure you include these items in your budget as living expenses because that's what they are. A common mistake people make is to forget to include these. As a result, they understate their total outgo.

What if we overestimate or underestimate our income for the year?

If during the year you see your income is going to be less than projected, you need to adjust your living expenses accordingly unless the margin amount you set aside (savings) is enough to offset the reduction. This is another good reason to have an annual cushion and to not spend all that you make.

Remember, though, that a reduction in income isn't usually dollar-for-dollar. If your income goes down $1, for instance, the reduction is really only a percentage of that, depending on your tax bracket. If you're in a 30-percent bracket, your taxes will go down $.30, so your living expenses will only need to be reduced by 70 cents.

If your income is more than projected, great! Just don't spend more than 70 percent of the increase or you will be in trouble when it comes to paying your annual taxes. Also, you may be moved into a higher tax bracket, so check that with your accountant before you make spending plans.

And remember, if your income goes up, you can always add that increase to savings or to your charitable giving. Don't automatically opt for a more opulent lifestyle. If you always increase living expenses as your income goes up, you will never accumulate the savings necessary for long-term financial independence.

What if we're running out of money before the end of the month?

There are only two possibilities. Either you don't have realistic amounts allocated for expenses and need to increase them or you have set realistic amounts and just aren't controlling them. In either case, you need to track the details for a while to see exactly where your money is going so you can either adjust the funds allocated or cut back on your spending.

What are some the major budget breakers to watch for?

Budget breakers are generally found among discretionary budget items. These items are primarily gifts, clothing, vacation, house furnishings, miscellaneous cash, and allowance.

It's interesting to note that the nondiscretionary items (fixed expenses such as utilities, mortgage, and gas for vehicles) very seldom are culprits. It's also interesting that most expenses in the budget are fixed. So the key to avoiding budget breakers is to control the half dozen or so unfixed expenses that tend to blow the budget. (Of course, if your fixed expenses are too high, perhaps you're in a house that is too much for your income or have car payments you can't handle, then they will contribute to your budget problems.) Julie and I have found that if we control vacation and gift spending, we're generally okay.

Is there an amount that is "too much" for Christians to have and use for living expenses?

As with many areas of the Christian life, it would be much easier if there were definitive answers. Then we could say that with a set amount of income, a person should only spend X amount for living expenses. But there is no such answer. God allows us a large area of freedom in the lifestyle area. He gives us these definitive boundaries: spend less than you make, give to the Lord, pay your taxes. Once we do these things, the amount left over is ours to do with as the Lord leads. Maybe we should give more. Maybe we should increase our standard of living. This matter is between the Lord and you. As long as you seek His direction and wisdom and are tuned in to His desires, you're free in this area.

Many people would like to tell you what is right for your life. But no matter where you draw the line, it's never an absolute. You may strive for a simpler lifestyle, but how simple is simple? No matter how much you reduce your lifestyle, it's likely someone in the world has a simpler one. Downward mobility isn't necessarily next to godliness. Neither is opulence. No matter how much you strive to elevate your lifestyle, someone in the world likely has a higher standard of living. The best answer and choice is simply to walk with God daily and ask Him for wisdom. He will freely give it.

Accountability in this area will also help make sure you're on track. What do I mean by accountability? Having someone in your life you know will shoot straight with you regarding your budget. Left to ourselves, we can justify any amount as "needed" in an expense category. Therefore, it's helpful to have someone periodically check our thinking for realism and balance. Julie and I have such a person in our lives. He helps us keep a good balance between giving, living, debt payments, and so on.

Game Plan

1. Do you and your spouse have a good budget system?

2. What is the most difficult problem you encounter in budgeting?

3. Have you made the distinction between monthly and non-monthly expenses? How will the concept of monthly versus non-monthly help your budget planning?

4. Do you and your spouse both give input when planning and modifying the budget?

5. Do you have one checking account or two? Explain why.

Chapter 9

The Banker Is Calling

Rob and Sarah were making headway on their financial planning. They agreed on how they would set their budget amounts and who would pay the bills. They decided it didn't make sense at this time for Sarah to go back to work. The next decision, though, opened up some wounds and proved to be difficult to talk about.

Decision 5: How Much Debt Should We Allow?

Sarah could tell from Rob's body language that he was less than enthusiastic about discussing their debt load. She was sure the memory of last Christmas was still too fresh.

She was correct. Rob was, indeed, replaying that holiday time in his mind.

Rob had been planning all year to surprise his family with the vacation of their dreams. A week skiing together in Colorado would make wonderful memories. No one could argue against that kind of investment, he reasoned.

Although it had been a tight year for them financially and he had to borrow money to pay for the trip, Rob knew the surprised and excited looks on his children's faces would be worth it. And besides, he figured he'd shown wise stewardship by using their home equity line of credit so the interest would be deductible on their taxes. The vacation costs wouldn't add that much debt to the house payments, and he was sure he could handle the additional monthly payments based on his projected salary. He couldn't wait to see everyone's faces when they opened their gift certificates Christmas morning.

As expected, the kids were overjoyed! It felt great to hear them call him "awesome" and "cool." He soon noticed, however, that Sarah wasn't quite as excited. In fact, she seemed almost on the verge of tears. Later that evening when they were alone, he cautiously broached the subject. "You don't seem very excited about the ski trip, Sarah…"

"Rob, it's not that I wouldn't love to go skiing with you and the kids. It's just that I know we don't have the money for such a luxury."

"I know it's a bit extravagant, honey. But I tapped into the home equity line of credit we set up a while back so we can at least deduct the interest and save on our tax bill."

"But, Rob, you know how much I hate being in debt—especially more debt on the house. Oh, honey, I know you wanted to do something special for us—especially since you've been working so many late nights—but I don't feel good about this."

"Well, it's done now, so you're just going to have to deal with it," Rob said.

Why did Sarah respond like she did? Why did Rob feel okay about the additional debt used for the vacation? We'll unpack the answers to these questions as we consider:

- reasons why debt has become so common and accepted
- how and why husbands and wives often respond differently to debt
- action steps for avoiding or getting out of debt

Reasons for Incurring Debt

Borrowing seems like the thing to do. Everyone does it. Dave Ramsey, author of *The Total Money Makeover,* says: "Debt is so ingrained into our culture that most Americans can't even envision a car without a payment, a house without a mortgage, a student without a loan, and credit without a card."[1] In preparing a financial plan for a client, it's necessary to determine assets and liabilities. Before I can help the client, I need to know what he owes and what he owns. Numerous times I've asked a client whether he has any debt and he's replied, "No. Well, except the home mortgage." We have gone so far in our thinking on borrowing that we don't consider what we owe on a home debt!

> *Anytime we go into debt, we're stealing from our future.*

The concept of using other people's money (OPM) has been taught in business schools for years. After all, if you can use other people's money and, with inflation, pay it back with cheaper dollars later, why not? You can get more bang for your buck now. This thinking satisfies our insatiable desire to have more than what we can afford. It's believing that what Scripture calls "the lust of the eyes [greedy longings of the mind]" can be satiated by more and we go into debt to get it (1 John 2:1 AMP, brackets in original).

Instead of saving for a larger down payment on a house to assume less debt, we do as we're told by the world. We stretch ourselves and acquire the maximum loan available to make the purchase. We unwisely presume we can easily pay it back or count on pay raises or bonuses for debt repayment. But anytime we do this, we're stealing from our future and sentencing ourselves to a lower lifestyle when we get there.

> *It's three times as hard to get out of debt as it is to get into debt.*

Debt is a subtle trap. A couple may be sticking close to their budget and only overspending by $20 a week, but over the course of a year this adds up to more than $1,000! Over several years, that $20 a week adds up to several thousand dollars and can create a significant debt problem. What started out as a very minor overspending problem ends up being a huge debt that's difficult to overcome.

Why is debt so hard to overcome? Say I overspend by $1,000 a year for ten years so I owe $10,000. Assuming a 10 percent interest rate, I will have to reduce my standard of living $3,000 the first year to get out of debt. How did I get the $3,000? First, I have to quit overspending the $1,000 (which is the piece most forget) a year. Then I need $1,000 to pay the interest and another $1,000 to pay down the principal at $1,000 per year. So what seemed to be a minor problem of overspending $1,000 a year ($20 a week) now causes me to reduce my lifestyle by $3,000 a year. It's three times as hard to get out of debt as it is to get into debt. This is the subtle trap of debt.

Debt is also hard to reduce because it must be paid back with after-tax dollars. If I owe $4,000 and am in a 33 percent tax bracket, I must earn $6,000 to have $4,000 left over to pay the debt. It's hard enough for most couples to make ends meet without debt exacerbating the problem.

Lending institutions and television advertisements contribute to the lure of debt with comments like these:

- "With a home equity loan you don't have to wait until 'someday' to travel…you can do it *now*!"
- "Repayment is comfortable with a minimum monthly payment."
- "You can arrange to pay 'interest only' for five years."

It's hard to be content when the world bombards us with "allegedly" risk-free ways to get what we want now even though we don't have the money. What lies are being promoted? "We deserve more." "It won't hurt." "If you don't make enough, it's okay. Go ahead and get it. You can pay it back later." As we discovered, however, "paying later" is extremely difficult. Debt and overspending always reduce our lifestyle in the future.

To live debt-free may require a radical lifestyle change. Julie and I found it required living in a smaller house longer, driving our older cars a few more years, and going camping instead of taking expensive vacations. When you decide to get out of debt or stay out of debt, you will likely have to forgo some current desires to attain rewards and benefits in the future. It will likely require looking a little different than your neighbors (and the world).

Another reason people take on debt is the husband's drive to provide. God has placed within each man a powerful drive to provide for his family. With this drive typically comes greater risk tolerance—an aptitude for risk taking. A husband may assume large debt loads to better care for and protect his family. He may want to provide a bigger house in a gated community, a larger SUV for his family's safety, and so on. He reasons that on his income he can take care of the debt. He may rationalize that even in the worst-case scenario (bankruptcy), he can always start over.

The wife often sees debt quite differently. It may be a tremendous threat to her bedrock need of security and comfort.

A couple would be wise to discuss how they individually feel about debt, the reasons acceptable for going into debt, the different types of debt, and if they choose to go into debt, how they plan to repay it.

Since men tend to show love by doing, they are inclined to buy "things" for the people they care about. In Rob's case, he planned an expensive family vacation. Gifts are great displays of love, but if debt is used to finance them, there could be unintended consequences. The wife may not see the possessions or activities as displays of love. In fact, she may view them as detriments—a threat to her security and the security of her children. She reasons that if her husband loves her, he won't jeopardize their ability to create a stable home for the family.

The next reason for taking on debt is that one of the spouses is discontent or wants to impress others. Sometimes the husband is discontent, so he takes on debt to try to find satisfaction. If he doesn't have a good self-image or a good understanding of true success, he may use debt to appear affluent and enhance his identity. Debt can allow people to *look* successful by the world's definition, when all the while they're barely getting by.

A wife's attitude may also contribute to the problem. Unknowingly she can encourage her husband to take on more debt than he would like because of her casual comments about wanting or needing something that is outside the budget. I remember a friend who took on a lot more debt because his wife kept saying, "I wish we had new curtains"; "We can't entertain until we redecorate"; "It's embarrassing to pick the children up in this old car"; "This apartment is no place for children—we need a house"; and "This carpet is sure getting worn." Although these comments seemed innocuous, they were sending a message to the husband that he wasn't providing enough. She wanted more, and without knowing it she was jeopardizing her basic security and comfort.

A wife, like her husband, can overspend if she has a poor self-image and is trying to impress others. Also, if she is angry at her husband or is trying to get his attention, she may spend extravagantly.

Once debt exists in a marriage or if you're considering taking on debt, it's important to be aware of the different responses of men and women.

A Husband's Response to Having Debt

The husband may overwork. He knows he needs to service the debt, so he justifies his long hours at work by saying, or at least thinking, "I have to work harder because of our large debt load."

His working more and more hours is usually not the response the wife is looking for. Time with him is how she feels loved, and if he's not around as much, she doesn't feel as loved. What seemed to be "just a debt problem" has now crept into a marriage problem. He feels he is showing love by the extra work hours he's putting in to provide, but she doesn't receive his efforts that way.

The husband may stop telling his wife what he's doing regarding debt. He doesn't let her know when he takes on more debt or why. He knows she will likely react negatively about debt, and he doesn't want to deal with it.

He doesn't understand her security orientation versus his risk-taking mindset. Many times I've been in meetings with a couple, and as we're going through the assets and liabilities, the wife will exclaim, "I didn't know we owed that!" Her husband had stopped communicating regarding debt because he was tired of her negative responses. Rather than try to explain his reasoning, and exhibit sensitivity for her need for security, he said nothing to his wife.

The husband may experience spiritual ups and downs when the debt load increases. As I've worked with couples, I've noticed that if a man's career is going well (income, promotions, recognition), debt tends to not be a big issue. It doesn't seem to affect the man's well-being spiritually. However, financial pressure tends to strip off our masks. What lies underneath is sometimes frustration, bitterness, and even anger. His frustration may be compounded because his options and flexibility are reduced. Proverbs 22:7 is true. The borrower does become the lender's slave. Add to that more work hours and, therefore, less time spent in Bible study, prayer, and in fellowship with other believers, and it's not pretty.

The husband may take on an attitude of "The debt is her fault" and assume no personal responsibility. He concludes that he's been driven to take out an inordinate amount of debt to satisfy his wife's desire for possessions or a certain lifestyle. He may not feel any personal responsibility and develop an attitude of apathy toward paying back the debt. His wife's security is of little concern to him.

A Wife's Response to Having Debt

The wife may become anxious about the debt. Because of a woman's basic nurturing instincts, she desires a secure environment. She likes to move into a house and put down roots. She often doesn't like to move around a lot. Debt threatens her security because she knows if the income isn't available to make the debt payments, she may have to relocate or even lose her home.

This anxiety could lead to devastating consequences. This was made very clear in a recent letter I received. The woman wrote, "I couldn't cope with the stress of my husband's attitude toward indebtedness. When I couldn't convince him of the disaster his spending could bring, for security of my home I had to legally cut our ties (my fear, of course, was that eventually we could lose our home). It was absolutely the most devastating experience ever." This woman was so fearful of losing her home because of the debt her husband was taking on that she went to the extreme of seeking divorce to make her environment secure.

I remember my wife's response when I casually mentioned we were establishing a line of credit for our firm to manage the ups and downs of seasonal cash flows. As a partner, I would be liable for my pro-rata share. Needless to say, I hadn't planned on the two-hour discussion that followed my comment! All of Julie's uneasiness about debt came to the surface. Why did we need a line of credit? Could we handle the debt?

What if our income went down? What about our home? What was the difference between having debt on the business and using credit cards?

I quickly realized that Julie's response to debt was very different from my response. I looked at it as a wise business move, a prudent decision based on sound facts. She saw her security threatened, and she didn't like it. It was then my responsibility to help her understand and get comfortable with the reasons for the debt, the amount of risk to us, and the probability of the debt getting out of hand. Her anxiety level was reduced because I talked it through with her.

The wife may nag her husband about the debt. An insecure wife may continually push her husband regarding their debt. The woman who wrote the letter stated that "when she couldn't convince him…" It's likely that she'd been nagging him about the debt to get him to think the way she did about it or at least communicate with her about it.

Nagging can be a cry for communication, but it can also be the result of the wife's lack of understanding on how debt is perceived by her husband. The letter writer revealed that she may not have understood how her husband perceived debt when she said, "I could not cope with the stress of my husband's attitude toward indebtedness…"

It could be that the husband was careless in his indebtedness; however, it's also possible that both of them simply didn't understand the way the other spouse perceived debt. Perhaps the husband was operating out of his provision drive, and the wife didn't know or understand that. Unfortunately, the "solution" for that couple was divorce. What a tragedy! We need to understand the different ways we perceive debt and seek to develop clear communication on the subject for the benefit of our marriages.

The wife could become apathetic about debt. She feels there's no reason for her to watch her small expenditures on clothes, gifts, and the kids because her husband is spending significant amounts on houses, boats, investments, and hobbies. She feels it's pointless to watch what she spends and stay within the budget when he doesn't. So she gives up and takes on debt for the things she wants.

Husbands: If your wife is indifferent about debt, that's a sign something's not right. Her bias toward security should typically cause her to have an aversion toward debt. So why would a wife become indifferent?

Is she using credit cards to buy things to make her happy and meet her needs because the husband is not? Is she trying to get his attention? Is she trying to get back at him for a slight? A wise husband will watch for these indicators and work to understand the "why" behind them. It's my experience that the real issue is never about money but about something deeper in the relationship.

The wife may lose respect for her husband when debt is taken on. This disrespect results because she doesn't feel he really cares about her since he's not listening to her input and he's willing to threaten her basic security by owing money. Since he doesn't explain the purpose of the debt to her, she may feel he doesn't know what he's doing. This causes her respect to wane even more, and she may start belittling or tearing him down. She reasons that if he really cared for her, he would discuss their debt situation and definitely not increase their debt load.

Action Steps for Dealing with Debt

How do we deal with these potential responses to debt in a marriage relationship? The following solutions are offered for your consideration.

First, the wife needs to be very careful not to destroy the provision drive of her husband. She needs to realize that this God-given drive to provide brings with it a higher risk tolerance than she probably has. She also needs to understand that debt wisely used in the establishment of a business and the growth of a husband's capital base will probably be a part of his life. She needs to be careful not to nag him about debt as he provides for her.

Both spouses need to understand the two types of debt:

- *Business-type or investment debt.* This is debt where the after-tax return is greater than the after-tax cost. This use of debt can be a viable part of a person's financial situation. This usually involves real estate or business.

- *Consumptive-type debt.* Particularly devastating in a marriage relationship is consumptive-type debt. This is debt for goods, such as furniture, cars, and boats. The after-tax cost is greater than the after-tax return (depreciation-type debt, where we can't sell an item for what we paid for it).

Understanding these two types of debt was the topic of my two-hour discussion with Julie. As you recall, she was concerned about my firm's establishing a line of credit. She was anxious about the impact of debt, wanting to know why and where it fit into our financial plan. It was my responsibility to help her be comfortable with these issues and clearly understand buisness debt versus consumptive debt so she could give me her insights.

A husband should seek and value his wife's input. Whether I take out the debt or not is secondary to including my wife in my thought process and getting her input. After talking it through with her, I may still choose to take out the loan, but I'm ultimately responsible to God for how I provide for my family and the financial decisions I make (1 Timothy 5:8).

Regarding getting the wife's input on debt, it's important to look at a side issue that's close to the hearts of all women: the home. Since the home is the wife's "territory," the way it's perceived is key to marriage harmony. It needs to be established that debt on the home is personal debt—not business or investment debt. The home should not be looked at as an investment.

Although the home will likely appreciate and have good growth in value when sold, it is sacred territory for the wife—a place where memories are made and where the family feels safe. The home should not be risked by home equity loans, second mortgages, or funding business or investment objectives unless agreed on by both husband and wife.

Husbands take note: When deciding how much debt to put on the home, ask these questions. Would we be more anxious and frustrated if we lived in a smaller house and our income went up so we could support a larger house later or if we lived in a larger house and our income went down to the point that we couldn't pay the mortgage payments and might lose the house? Your answer to these two scenarios will give you insights into your risk tolerance.

I remember the look on the face of a client's wife when she realized her home was lost. All the investments her husband had made had gone bad, and the home had been leveraged. What she cared about was being ripped away. Yes, they would have been worth a lot more had the investments worked out, but was that worth the risk of losing their home? My observation was that to the wife it was not.

I strongly recommend that a debt-free house should be pursued aggressively. Paying off your home may seem an odd thing to do in this age of putting off payments, but it is a great thing to do for your marriage!

Couples should have a strategy in place to handle major purchases. If provision isn't made for major purchases, debt is usually the method used. Each couple needs to define what constitutes a "major purchase" for them, but in general a major purchase is any purchase that's not part of the normal living expenses. They are typically more expensive items, including furniture, cars, golf clubs, boats, vacation homes, and home improvements. Julie and I have found that defining what we consider major purchases and then communicating about them *before* any purchase is made makes our marriage more harmonious.

> *Having a plan for major purchases will eliminate much potential conflict in your marriage.*

A lot of conflict in marriage is a result of money being spent and debts incurred that were not agreed upon between husband and wife. Imagine how a wife would react if her husband came home with a $500 set of golf clubs and proudly told her how much he needed them. Or perhaps a wife proudly displayed an expensive new coat to her husband. In both cases it won't be the items themselves that cause a rift but the lack of communication and agreement on the debt incurred to purchase them.

Having a plan for major purchases will eliminate much potential conflict in your marriage because it promotes discussion and, in most cases, sets limits on the use of debt.

A couple should practice gratitude. Periodically sit down together and make a list of all you have to be thankful for. This is a practical way to learn to be content. It helps to get your focus off the world (the lust of the eyes) and back on God and what He has blessed you with. We need to quit thinking about what we don't have. We come into this world with nothing, and we leave with nothing (1 Timothy 6:7). We are not entitled to a certain amount of material possessions. This perspective will typically act as a governor on the accumulation of debt. It will also help maintain a more balanced perspective. Julie and I do this frequently, especially when we are tempted to buy something. We reflect on all we have that we wouldn't take money for.

Getting Out of Debt

This chapter wouldn't be complete without some practical steps on how to tackle existing debt. Here are some suggested steps.

- Evaluate your income and the four main areas of money use (living expenses, taxes, giving, and debt payments) to ensure you have a positive margin. Many people continue to go deeper in debt because they have no financial plan. They have never determined if they're living within their income. The first step, then, is to make sure you aren't accumulating more debt by overspending.

- Implement a cash-flow control system that enables you to accomplish your spending plan (see chapter 8). A good control system will help ensure that you accumulate a positive cash-flow margin.

- Once you have a positive cash-flow margin, those funds can be used to reduce your debt. As your debt reduces, you have more margin, and the positive cycle continues.

- As well as the preceding steps, if you feel you need to do something drastic:
  - Sell an asset. This might be a car; a television; or stocks, bonds, and other investments.
  - Downsize your house.
  - Put your children in public school or homeschool (versus private school).
  - Cut up your credit cards. They encourage overspending. Remove the temptation and enhance your positive cash-flow margin.

- *Warning:* Do not consolidate your loans. This doesn't solve the problem. Consolidation may reduce your monthly debt payment, but it also means you're not paying your debt off as quickly as possible. Without a financial plan, the extra money that was being used for debt repayment may well be spent in other ways so your debt grows. It's far better to "bite the bullet" and address your debt problem rather than making it "easier" through loan consolidation and paying less on the amount owed. Debts need to be paid, and the sooner the better.

Conclusion

It was helpful for Rob and Sarah to reflect on their different perspectives of debt. Rob gained a better understanding regarding Sarah's response on the Christmas ski trip, and he agreed to do better about getting her input before taking on more debt. Sarah committed to being more encouraging to Rob regarding his income level. She wanted him to know she didn't want him to ever feel pressured to take on debt because of any possible discontent on her part. She also let him know she would work on appreciating his risk-taking bent. Sarah told Rob she was grateful for all the decisions he'd made to keep them financially stable.

What about you? Do you and your spouse need to stop right now and do what Sarah and Rob did? Why not talk about your answers to this question: "What is my attitude toward debt?" This is a great place to start building harmony about finances in your relationship.

Game Plan

1. Are the things you would like to buy on credit worth it in light of keeping harmony in your marriage?

2. Do both of you communicate about finances before making major purchases?

3. What debts do you have now? Why do you have them?

4. If you don't own your home, what steps can you take to accelerate paying it off?

5. Should you cut up your credit cards? Why or why not?

Chapter 10

But It's Such a Good Deal!

Rob and Sarah felt much better after their talk on debt. Finances had been an elephant in the room for a long time, so they were glad to have that decision behind them. They were encouraged that the next discussion had to do with investments.

Decision 6: How Do We Decide Which Investments to Make?

Rob and Sarah's differences on investment opportunities had become painfully obvious several years ago. Rob encountered Sam, an old friend from college, who wanted to get Rob involved in a "deal of a lifetime."

"Sarah, do you remember the situation with Sam?" asked Rob.

"How could I forget?" Sarah replied.

"I know. I remember when Sam met with me. He said, 'Rob, I've just come across a super deal I know you'll be interested in. For an investment of only $20,000 you can double it to $40,000 in the next two years! I've done a lot of research on it, and both the concept and people behind it seem to be sound. It's a no-lose opportunity!' And since Sam had been my friend for a long time, I was sure if he was excited about something it must be a good deal."

Rob had contemplated Sam's deal and got more and more excited about the opportunity. He'd been working hard at his job and had accumulated $25,000 in savings. The money was earmarked for the kids' education fund and for a new car. As Rob thought about it though, he realized they could get two cars with the $20,000 they'd earn and still put money into the college fund. He knew Sarah would be happy if she had an SUV for all the carpooling she did. Having convinced himself it was worth looking into, he met with his friend. "Sam, I'm always interested in anything that can make me money. What is it?"

Sam shared the details and his excitement. That information, combined with Rob's ability to imagine what he could do with the $45,000 in only two years, was enough. Rob decided to make the investment. That night he tried to get Sarah onboard and even shared all the numbers with her. But Sarah hadn't been convinced. She didn't want to dip into their savings. She asked Rob all kinds of questions about the investment, some of which he couldn't answer.

Despite Sarah's skepticism, Rob moved ahead with the investment. But it didn't turn out as projected. Rob and Sarah were fortunate to get back half of their investment, but that meant they had to put off getting a newer car for two more years. That one investment decision put a lot of stress on their marriage.

Reasons Investments Can Cause Marital Conflict

Investments! Other than debt, no area of a couple's finances can evoke more conflict. Let's look at three reasons why this is the case.

Foundational Male/Female Differences

Let's unpack the investment situation Rob and Sarah experienced to see how the differences can play out.

Rob exhibited his God-given drive to provide and the tendency to put his identity in his wealth. Like most men, Rob is attracted to investments because it's another way to generate income to provide for his family and build wealth (and thus, his identity). This is why men often have their antennae up and enjoy coming up with one good deal after another. If a husband isn't careful, however, the drive to provide can easily be replaced by greed. Satan is an expert at taking a good thing, such as provision, and corrupting it. "Greed" is a "covetous drive or longing to have something." It's especially evident in the desire to get something for nothing or next to nothing. Greed is the underlying motivation that makes the "get rich quick" schemes so popular. It can blind us to the true facts of a deal. Greed is also a barrier that can cause a husband to shut out the counsel of his wife even when she sends him loud and clear warning signals.

This happened with Rob. Instead of questioning the amazing return potential on the investment, which should have been a warning sign (earning $20,000 in two years would require an annualized return of 36 percent!), Rob rationalized why it must be a good deal. After all, he respected his friend Sam. "If Sam feels it is a good deal, it must be." Even though Sarah was uncomfortable, Rob didn't put much credence in what she said because she didn't know the facts or what a good man Sam was. This brings us to the next difference in the typical male/female approach to investments.

Rob and Sarah exhibited their logical and intuitive natures. Men tend to be logical. They look at the numbers, calculate, do risk analyses, and figure the probabilities. A man believes the numbers are all there is to the investment. Women tend to rely on intuition. Sarah responded to Rob negatively because "she didn't feel good about it."

This blows a man's circuits. He doesn't understand what the woman means when she says she doesn't "feel" good about something. He wants to know *why* she feels that way. He wants facts and figures.

Then the woman gets defensive. She doesn't know why she feels the way she does, she just does. This "feeling" is her God-given intuition.

Rob would have been well advised to give credence to Sarah's concern even though she offered no factual reason. Intuition has saved many people from disastrous investments. I like this comment by Frontier Airlines Captain Chick Stevens:

> I am for example, nonplussed by [women's] ability to understand things without having knowledge of those things. A sort of swift and sure instinct which leaps directly from problem to conclusion without being confused by facts. We males are bound by our inherent natures to cope with facts—great bespatterings of facts—wending our way to conclusions brings these facts into regimented order. We are pushed

just a bit off center when, after performing our labors of sorting, ana-lyzing, weighing, assigning degrees of importance, we reach our con-clusion to find our women already there, smiling sweetly.[1]

Sarah's security orientation was highlighted. She might have been hes-itant because she didn't want to lose the security of the $25,000 in savings. Rob needed to realize that his risk-taking mindset might be foreign to his wife. Instead of trying to make her think the same way he did, he should have taken the time to discover her concerns and address them before making a decision.

Rob and Sarah exhibited the male/female differences in long-term versus short-term time horizons. Sarah might have been cautious because she likes seeing the cash in the bank now. It's difficult for her to feel as comfortable with a potential $40,000 in the bank in two years. Her ori-entation is more for the here and now. It goes against her nature to want to take $20,000 and invest it now to *maybe* have more in the future.

I've found that because of the desire for security and short-term ori-entation, wives are usually more interested in cash and liquid invest-ments (easily convertible to cash) than in nonliquid investments. I recall a discussion Julie and I had about rental real estate properties. I spent a couple of hours discussing with her the benefits of tax savings, appre-ciation, and income from the investment. Her response was one of extreme caution. She asked, "What if the renters don't pay, and we need to make the mortgage payment?" and "What if we have a lot of repairs and upkeep that takes our cash?" It became obvious as we talked that she was much more comfortable with liquidity and cash than with the unknowns of rental property ownership. (So did I go ahead and make the real estate investment? You'll find out later in this chapter.)

Another reason women tend to prefer cash and liquidity is because, in most cases, they are dealing with short-term uses of money—kids' clothes, braces, groceries, and the like. They know intuitively that these things can't be bought with nonliquid investments.

Before leaving this discussion of differences, let me add that even though my illustrations presuppose that women aren't interested in investments, which is often the case, there are situations that may pique a woman's interest. If her husband is slothful and not meeting the family's needs, a wife may be assertive with investments. If a wife isn't content to live within her husband's income, she may become interested in investments as a way to get more of the things she needs or wants. If she's detail oriented, she may be attracted to investments and the challenge of understanding them. Her family background may also contribute to a heightened interest level. If her parents had an interest in investments, she may have participated in the decision-making process, thus having wonderful memories of connecting with them in that way.

Lack of Communication

More often than not, the husband doesn't want to talk to his wife about the investment and just goes ahead and does it. He feels he knows more about the numbers than she does, so he is more qualified to make the decision. This was Rob's thinking. "So why bother her?" he reasons. He might also have learned that when he does talk to her, he can't get her to think the way he does so he would just as soon not fight the battle. He may also feel the openness would make him too vulnerable to failure in her eyes. He's afraid he'll hear "I told you so" if the investment fails.

Instead of trying to make his wife think the way he does, a husband should talk to her and ask for her input. It's an understatement to say that much conflict results when the husband doesn't communicate with his wife and, instead, just calls up and says, "Honey, I just made this great investment for $20,000! We'll earn $20,000 from it in two years."

Just the fact that the husband wants his wife's input honors her and goes a long way toward promoting marital harmony.

Pressure to Increase Income

The pressure to increase income can lead to an unhealthy focus on investments from either the husband or the wife. As noted, the husband could put pressure on himself to make more money because of a wrong perspective of success. He could take more risk to try for more rewards (more money) to feel better about himself because his identity is in his net worth.

If the wife isn't content with the family income, she could pressure her husband to provide more. This pressure may incline him to look for investments that promise to generate a lot of money very quickly. His self-image may be damaged if he can't make enough to please her, so he seeks more and more agressive investment opportunities.

Solving the Conflict

To avoid potential conflicts created by investments, consider taking these steps.

Examine Your Motives

Husbands, take the time to evaluate your motives. Are you pursuing the investment because of greed? The Bible contains very clear warnings about the outcome of investments if gain is the motive:

- "A faithful man will abound with blessings, but he who makes haste to be rich will not go unpunished" (Proverbs 28:20).
- "A man with an evil eye hastens after wealth and does not know that want will come upon him" (28:22).

Evaluate Your Contentment Level

Both husband and wife need to regularly evaluate their contentment level. The husband may be prone to pride and the need to impress; thus, he may tend to overspend or take unwise investment risks. A wife may be overtly or subtly expressing discontentment and pressuring her husband to make more, which could lead him to take higher risks. Scripture reminds us: "Make sure that your character is free from the love of money, being *content* with what you have; for He Himself has said, 'I will never desert you, nor will I ever forsake you'" (Hebrews 13:5).

Communicate Clearly

Husbands, it's crucial that you get your wives' input before making any investment decision. Even though her intuitive reasoning about the investment may not make sense to your way of thinking, *you need to listen to her.*

> ***If you, the husband, don't understand the investment well
> enough to explain it to your wife, then don't invest.***

My observation is that in most cases the wife just wants to make
sure she has input and feels her husband is communicating with her.
I'm convinced that a husband's final decision regarding the investment
is much less of an issue to his wife than whether the husband took the
time to get his wife's input. I've found that once I get Julie's input, I have
much greater freedom to make the decision. Without her input on an
investment it seems we're always at a point of conflict.

I remember showing up for a client meeting that I assumed would
be with just the husband. Much to my surprise, when I walked into his
office his wife met me. When I expressed my surprise that she was there
for the meeting, she said, "This is the only way I can get filled in on what
is going on. He talks to you!"

A general rule of thumb about investments is that if you (the husband) don't understand the investment well enough to explain it to your
wife, then don't invest. Rob should have been able to answer *all* of Sarah's questions about Sam's "great opportunity." Since he couldn't, that
should have been a red flag regarding that particular investment.

> ***Most wives would rather take less risk and have less in the future if
> it means more short-term security.***

Because your wife likely has a short-term focus on investments,
sharing your long-term view will probably be helpful. Sound financial
planning requires diversification and a long-term perspective, and thus
mandates a move into investment vehicles other than cash. This perspective may be natural for you, but it may not be for your wife. Most
women will follow their short-term focus and be most content with
investments like cash, money market funds, and so on.

It's your job as husband to help your wife see the long-term benefits
of the investment and where it fits into your overall financial plan. All
the while, however, remain quite sensitive to the short-term needs that
must be met. It's these short-term needs that men so often overlook. In

your zeal for providing for the future—education, retirement, repayment of debt—you may neglect the need for drapes, kids' school clothes, activity fees, and the like. For the sake of your marriage, any investment decision needs to factor in the family's short-term needs. You will be well advised not to ignore the pressures your wife is feeling in the short term. Most wives would rather take less risk and have less in the future if it means more short-term security.

I've found that one of the most effective ways to ensure that Julie and I balance her short-term focus with my long-term focus is to ask her for her priority uses of our margin. In other words, what would she prefer to do with the difference between our earnings and our expenses? Because of my long-term mentality, I'm naturally thinking of investments and savings to the potential exclusion of all other uses of money. Julie, on the other hand, is likely thinking of short-term uses that may be more practical. For instance, when our boys were growing up, she responded to my question about uses for our cash by saying she would like to have more put into the vacation category (her parents live in Phoenix, and she liked taking the boys to visit their grandparents often). She also was interested in getting a different car sooner than I was planning.

It's not that she was right or that I was right. The point is that I needed to factor what she was thinking into my decision making. If we have a margin of $3,000, I may have more harmony in my marriage if I put $1,000 of it into the vacation category of our budget and invest $2,000 of it. On the other hand, there are times I feel I should invest the entire $3,000. When this happens, I talk more with Julie about the purpose for the investment and my reasoning. This way of communicating has been very helpful for us.

Financial vs. Marital Risk

So how do husbands make investment decisions? After talking it through with our wives and getting their input, we then weigh the risk. After weighing the risk, we decide for or against. How do we weigh the risk? We consider two types of risk: *financial* and *marital*.

> ### *Marital risk is typically much greater than financial risk.*

Let's look at Rob's situation again. Rob knew Sarah was uncomfortable using education and car money to make the investment. The financial risk Rob faced was the same anyone faces with a 36-percent projected return. He stood a good chance of losing the money because risk and reward go together regarding investments. That high return had high risk…and thus a high probability of loss.

First, if Rob and Sarah had the money to lose, they could probably have withstood the financial risk. However, they did not have the extra money. Rob was investing their auto and education funds.

Second, Rob had not factored in the other major factor—marital risk. Marital risk is typically much greater than financial risk. It's one thing to lose the money; it's quite another to live in harmony with your wife after telling her you lost the money earmarked for a new family car and the kids' education.

Rob and Sarah had some baggage from that bad investment decision. Rob had to work longer hours to recoup the loss, and the family had to wait an extra couple of years for the new car. The result was additional stress on their marriage.

If Rob had been wiser, he would have discerned that Sarah would rather have a bird in her hand (the $20,000) than have two birds (the potential $40,000) in the bush. Rob would then have concluded that the investment was not worth the marital risk at their current savings level.

In any investment there is always trade-off and risk. The question is whether or not the risk is worth the reward. Too often we ask about risk strictly from a financial sense and forget that the greatest risk could be to our marriage relationship. To paraphrase Scripture, what does it profit a man if he amasses a lot of investments but loses his marriage and children? Investments should be evaluated from a financial standpoint as well as a "marriage harmony" standpoint.

Do you remember the rental property decision I discussed with Julie? I decided not to do it—primarily because of the time it would require to manage the property and the risk of depleting our cash reserves. I already had many demands on my time, and that investment would have required me to be on call 24 hours a day to fix things and deal with tenants. (I had three young sons who needed my time more than we needed that property investment.)

Potentially, we could have earned more money with property appreciation, tax benefits, and income with the rental property than we would on our savings account. However, the risk of the property not being rented and beginning to deplete our reserves was too great at that stage in our financial lives. I determined that the worst-case scenario with the property would put too much stress on our marriage and wasn't worth the potentially greater return.

This doesn't mean that a husband always has to do what his wife suggests regarding investments. She is to have input, and then he has the final decision. I would comment, however, that it seems wives are right more often than they're wrong.

Julie and I feel the simple policy of not committing to an investment without talking it over keeps us from responding to the lure of the moment and potentially making a decision we would later regret. I've also found that if I can and will answer her question, "Can we afford to lose this money?" I will have a lot more freedom in making the decision. If the answer is yes, her worries are reduced and her comfort level increased.

Once the decision is made, both husband and wife must resist the urge to say "I told you so" no matter how the investment turns out. The husband will be tempted to do this if he doesn't make the investment and it turns out to be a real winner. The wife will be tempted to utter this comment if he makes the investment and it goes badly. Remember, we're after harmony and communication. Investments are only a tool. They shouldn't become a source of arguing or tearing each other down.

Sound Knowledge About Investments

Many times the correct decision about investments will be made for you if you're thinking correctly. Let's look at some truths about investments.

Keep in mind realistic returns and the purpose of investments. In my business of financial planning, I often deal with individuals who have been making investments for 30 to 40 years. What becomes obvious is that a person doesn't become wealthy from investments. He gets wealthy by spending less than he makes from his vocation over a long period of time and preserving that surplus through investments. In other words, investments are "vehicles used for preservation of capital" and not for dramatic increases in capital. This being the case, we should be content with reasonable rates of return of zero to four percent (real rate) for five-year money investments and four to eight percent (real rate of return) for 10-year money investments. (Real rates of return are the returns on investments over inflation.)

Note: Are you questioning my claim that wealth is preserved and not created through investments? You may think about a guy you know who bought a piece of land for $1,000 an acre and sold it for a return of 200 percent. Or perhaps you're considering someone whose stock doubled three weeks after it went public. These people made money from their investments, didn't they? Although that *could* happen, it's my experience that in most cases that's *not* what happens. The person who makes a lot of money in land, for instance, is usually the one who deals in land frequently. That's his business. Therefore, he's generating income as a result of his vocation, not as a result of an investment. He just happens to be in a business that uses investment vehicles (land).

It's easy to confuse vocation with investment. As a result, we can be tempted to go out and buy land to try to make as much money as that fellow did, and then we're disappointed when that doesn't happen. The same is true with the man who had stock in the publicly traded company. He knows the company and has stock in it because that's his vocation. If it was easy to earn 200 percent or double your money in three weeks, everyone would do it. If an investment is a "sure thing," then your money isn't needed in the investment. Those who bring it to you would be doing it all themselves. This sets up the next principle.

Risk and reward go together. You should only invest in high return/ high risk investments with money you can afford to lose. *Getting rich quick doesn't work.* "He who gathers little by little will increase [his riches]" (Proverbs 13:11 AMP, brackets in original).

Investments are only tools. Investments shouldn't be purchased at the cost of harmony between the husband and wife. If the investment discourages unity in the marriage, don't do it!

Sequential investing is best. In Ron Blue's book *Master Your Money,* he highlights a simple-but-profound strategy that will help you (as a couple) avoid a lot of mistakes. Here are the steps:

> *Step 1:* Eliminate all credit card and consumer debt. This provides an immediate investment return of 12 to 21 percent, depending on the interest rate you're paying. This is the first use of any excess margin.
>
> *Step 2:* Set aside one month's living expenses in the checking account. This step ensures you have an amount to "prime the pump" for your cash-flow system.
>
> *Step 3:* Invest between 6 to 18 months' living expenses in an interest-bearing money market fund account. This is your emergency fund and is the critical step to ensure you do not go into debt during emergencies.
>
> *Step 4:* Save in an interest-bearing account for major purchases, such as automobiles, furniture, and home down payments.
>
> *Step 5:* Accumulate [cash] to meet long-term goals.[2]

Diversification is essential for preservation of capital. After you've implemented the steps just mentioned, you're ready to invest. At this point, I recommend you seek expert advice to help you develop a diversified investment plan in keeping with your goals, temperament, income, tax bracket, and age. Any plan should include fixed income investments (bonds, CDs, money market funds, treasury bills), equities (mutual funds and stocks), and real estate (raw land, income properties). The percentages will depend on the previously mentioned factors.

The biblical imperative for diversification is found in Ecclesiastes 11:1-2: "Cast your bread on the surface of the waters, for you will find it after many days. Divide your portion to seven, or even to eight, for you do not know what misfortune may occur on the earth."

As a general rule, don't make tax-motivated investments.

Investments must make economic sense. When considering an investment, ask these two questions: Does this investment have a good chance of generating income or appreciation? Is it an investment that will still be a strong asset for us 10 to 15 years from now?

In my business I have the privilege of seeing the financial statements of men and women who have been investing for many, many years. I know there are tried and true investments that stand the test of time and remain viable, long-term, economic values. I typically see stocks, bonds, cash, CDs, and real estate of all kinds on balance sheets. I typically do *not* see cattle deals, opal mines, energy deals, and the like that have value for only three or four years after the investment was made. The reason is that most of those types of investments were for tax reduction motives rather than being economic value motivated.

As a general rule, don't make tax-motivated investments. Your investment may have tax benefits, but that should not be the motivation. The investment should make economic sense first and foremost. Tax benefits are secondary. If you save $1,000 in taxes but lose $10,000 on the investment, you're not better off.

Do not borrow for an investment. Even if it looks like a great deal, an investment is not worth going into debt. As the saying goes, "If you can't afford to take the trip, don't buy the ticket." Nothing is worse than having to pay off the loan used on a worthless investment. Furthermore, if you borrow, you must be able to earn more on the investment than you're paying for the loan, and that requires additional risk. For example, why borrow money at five percent to try to earn more than five percent when if you just didn't borrow you would have the five-percent return risk free?

Never cosign for an investment. Without exception, my clients who have cosigned for people have suffered for it. In all my consulting, I have yet to see these verses *not* come true:

- "He who is guarantor for a stranger will surely suffer for it, but he who hates being a guarantor is secure" (Proverbs 11:15).
- "Do not be among those who give pledges, among those who become guarantors for debts" (22:26).

If an investment needs a co-signature or you need a cosigner for an investment, that's a sure indication you shouldn't be involved.

Do not get involved in a matter too great for you (Psalm 131:1). In other words, don't invest in something you don't know anything about. This could get a person in trouble in two ways. First, if he knows nothing about it, he would violate the principle of being able to explain it to his wife before making the investment. Second, he will likely not be able to ask the pertinent questions necessary for an effective evaluation.

There are enough quality investments available that you can understand. Avoid pursuing the ones you don't. A friend of mine recently found this truth out to the tune of $300,000. Instead of keeping his money in areas he was familiar with, he ventured into areas he knew little about. (If you insist on getting into an area you know little about, make sure you use money you can afford to lose because that's usually what happens.)

Conclusion

Rob and Sarah were excited about exploring the investment decision. The "Sam" investment experience had taught them a better way to process the investment possibilities that had come their way since then. With the information covered in "Decision 4: How Do We Set Budget Amounts," they were completely on the same page in this financial area. It was a nice way to end the day. Now they looked forward to a nice, relaxing dinner together.

Game Plan

1. As a husband, do you value your spouse's intuition when making investment decisions?

2. Recount a time you made a good investment. What process did you use?

3. Recount a time you made a bad investment. What did you do or not do that you now realize wasn't such a good idea?

4. How do your temperaments play into your investment decision making?

5. Do you know your spouse's priority for using your margin? In other words, what he or she prefers to invest in?

Chapter 11

To Give or Not to Give

Rob and Sarah felt the probing questions in the notebook had been helpful, and they now had some positive direction regarding handling finances. They were especially encouraged when, as they wrapped up the day on Saturday, they realized they were of one mind regarding investments. That realization, a nice dinner together, and good night's sleep had them refreshed and energized. They only had two more decisions to deal with, and it only seemed appropriate that they were discussing them on Sunday morning. They missed being at their home church, but they also knew this weekend had been long overdue and much needed.

"Well, only two more decisions to discuss," Rob said as he picked up the notebook from the bedside table. "Once we get through these, we'll be able to hit the road. We may even have time for lunch at that Riverside Café we passed coming up here."

"That would be great!" Sarah responded. She always enjoyed a meal out—especially because the kids' activities made getting out as a couple difficult. "But do you think we can afford it after all we've talked about?"

"That's why I want to do it on the way home," Rob explained. "Once we're home, this budgeting process will kick in, and we may never be able to eat out again." Rob smiled, laughed, and gave a playful tug on Sarah's shirt sleeve.

"So let's knock these decisions out of the way so we can get on the road," Sarah said.

Decision 7: How Much Should We Give?

Oh my! Why couldn't we have an easier topic on our last day, thought Sarah. Rob and I have always had differences in this area.

Sarah was the daughter of frugal parents who still gave generously to the church, to missionaries, and to those in need. Rob, on the other hand, grew up in a home where giving was mostly done at Thanksgiving and Christmas—if at all.

As a matter of fact, just last Sunday the pastor at their home church had talked about the new building program and challenged everyone to consider prayerfully how much they could give. Sarah had wanted to talk to Rob about it, but she hadn't broached the subject yet. She decided now was as good a time as any.

"Rob, do you remember the pastor's comments on giving last Sunday?"

"Yeah. Didn't he talk about the new building and contributing to the funding?" Rob responded. He shrugged.

"What did you think about what he said?"

"Oh, I don't know. It seems like the church never has enough money," Rob said. "If it isn't one thing, it's another. It's hard for me to get too excited about giving. It seems like a bottomless pit."

"They really do need the new education wing to meet the needs of all the children. You know our children will benefit too."

"Yeah, I know. It just seems like so much money. I'm not sure our little bit would help that much. And besides, I'm a little uncomfortable giving when things are already so tight for us."

"Did you hear what the pastor said about giving? How it's for our benefit…and how God commands it?"

"Yes, I heard him. I still don't want to give more than we already do. We give to the general fund a couple times a year. That should be enough."

"Honey, I really think we should give more. Don't you think we could pledge $3,000?"

"Sarah, you've got to be kidding! I just said I really don't want to give more, and you want to give $3,000! This always seems to happen. Every few months you get on me about giving more to the church. If it's not the building fund, it's the mission fund or something else. Can't you see that I really don't want to give away very much? I work too hard for it."

"Well, I'm sorry! I don't understand why you don't want to give like I do."

"Well, I don't, okay? Let's drop it."

Reasons a Husband Might Be a Hesitant Giver

One spouse being enthusiastic about giving and the other spouse being more hesitant or totally resistant is a common problem. In Sarah and Rob's case, Sarah is the giver and Rob is reluctant. It can go the other way too. The husband may have a generous bent whereas the wife is reticent. We'll look at reasons why each spouse might be hesitant to give. Let's start with the husband.

The husband's God-given drive to provide might interfere with giving. Giving cuts across the grain of provision. It's easy for a husband to rationalize his reticence to give by asking, "How can I provide for my family if we give the money I earn away?" He might also say, "I can provide better if we don't give so much away." Many men reason that it takes money to make money. If they give away any of their capital, it will be harder to generate income and create more capital because their investment base has been reduced.

> *Looking long-term can make the husband reluctant to give, and too often he doesn't share his reasons with his wife.*

A husband's provision drive should never be used as an excuse not to give. If you don't have a desire to give, it's time to ask yourself some questions. Are you tight with your money? Are you greedy? Do you have a poor self-image that you're trying to salve with your money? Do you lack appreciation for what God has done in your life? Are you hesitant to acknowledge God's hand in your life and in your finances? Giving—or lack of giving—is a good barometer of these things.

The husband's long-term perspective may hinder giving. The husband is typically looking down the road and knows he needs to have money saved for contingencies the wife may not be inclined to think about because of her shorter-term orientation. He is undoubtedly thinking about retirement and the kids' education. Or he may see a move coming that will require additional funds, the house is going to need painting, or inflation will require a slightly larger nest egg than originally planned. Looking long-term can make the husband reluctant to give, and too often he doesn't share his reasons with his wife. To avoid conflict over giving, he needs to tell her what he's thinking and what potential occurrences in the future have caused him to be resistant to giving.

A husband's lack of sensitivity may impact his willingness to give. Men tend to be less emotional and people-centered than women. This means women are more likely to be tuned in to the needs around them. A man's abstract, calculated, and somewhat insensitive makeup can lead him to overlook or be oblivious to needs.

Since a lot of giving is in response to appeals made by people, the wife may be more inclined to give than her husband. I know this is true with Julie and me. If someone asks us for money, she is more inclined to meet the need than I am. She sees past the need to the person and wants to help. My first response is to look at the need and figure out why it exists and if it is legitimate. I tend to care less about the individual behind the need because I focus on the facts.

Reasons a Wife Might Be a Hesitant Giver

The wife feels her security is threatened. Just as the man saw money as a source of capital and income, the wife sees it as security and comfort. If money is given away, it's not available to provide a stronger sense of security for her and the home. What if her husband loses his job? What if the car breaks down or the air conditioning needs replaced? What about the possibility of private school for the kids? How can we afford to buy curtains for the home or remodel the laundry room that needs it so badly? How will I be taken care of if my husband is giving our money away?

The wife likes to see the cash. In many cases the wife is responsible for the day-to-day expenses, such as clothes, groceries, and the kids' needs. If money is given away, she may be concerned she can't meet those needs. Having cash available in an emergency fund is comforting to her. I've observed that wives who are hesitant to give are not nearly as hesitant if a *noncash asset* is given away, such as real estate, stock, or a mutual fund.

I remember a meeting with a couple where the importance of cash was an issue in their giving decisions. Their net worth was $5 million, but most of it was tied up in land. The husband wanted to help a friend not lose his business. He wanted to give his friend $30,000. This wasn't a large amount in relation to his net worth, but it was a significant portion of his available cash. There were also some items for the home that his wife had been planning to get. The discussion was tense because the husband wanted to do something good, but he wasn't being sensitive to his wife's needs.

No matter how great the need for our money, our greatest need is to promote harmony and unity in our marriages. We need to be careful that when we give away our money we're not giving away our marriages as well.

The wife may be reluctant about giving because her husband doesn't communicate well. Perhaps her husband just drops on her his desire to give without discussing with her how it will affect the big picture. Most women will not fight giving if they're communicated with and understand that their security isn't being threatened with the gift. Communication is also critical to help understand where giving fits into the overall financial plan for the family.

Like their husbands, wives must be careful not to use these reasons as excuses not to give. Hesitancy about giving should lead a woman to look closely at her attitude. She may not be appreciative and thankful to God for all He has done and is doing in her life. She may have a poor self-image and, as a result, be trying to buy "position" among her peers. She may be greedy and selfish. She may not be growing spiritually so, as a result, her sensitivity to giving is not keen.

Reasons Both Husband and Wife Might Be Hesitant to Give

A couple who lacks spiritual maturity may be hesitant to give. Since giving is not a natural activity but a supernaturally inspired one, giving requires spiritual maturity on the part of the givers. Although non-Christians do give charitably to colleges, hospitals, and the like, my observation is that maximum giving results from being in close fellowship with God on a daily basis. If either spouse isn't growing spiritually, there may be some hesitation on that person's part when it comes to giving.

> *You should give at the level comfortable for the least spiritually mature spouse.*

It's not uncommon in a marriage relationship for one spouse to be further along on his or her spiritual journey than the other. It's important for each spouse to give the other the freedom to grow. With time and prayer, the other partner may come to the same level of desire for giving that the other is experiencing now.

A warning: Many times the more spiritual spouse may feel he or she must give to be in obedience to God. So this spouse may sneak around and give without telling the spouse. God doesn't need your money at the expense of your marriage. You should give at the level comfortable for the least spiritually mature spouse (what the spouse is comfortable with). Remember, you can also give gifts of time, counsel, meals, and such.

Poor giving decisions made in the past may affect current desires to give. Perhaps you gave someone money, and it was spent in a way you disagreed with or disapproved of. Perhaps you don't agree with some of the financial decisions made by the leaders of your church. Many of us have made bad financial investments and yet we don't stop investing. Just because we make a bad spiritual investment doesn't mean we should quit giving.

We need to remember that even though we're called to be wise and discerning, we don't always get it right. We should draw on our faith and trust God to fulfill His purposes through our giving.

Giving is hindered because one spouse has a "heart to give" and the other doesn't. One spouse may have the spiritual gift of giving or mercy and the other one doesn't. This isn't good or bad, but it needs to be understood as a potential reason for hesitancy on the part of a spouse. If both of you haven't taken a spiritual gifts test, I encourage you to do so. This will help both of you understand your gifts and your spouse's gifts and how they manifest. Here again, marriage harmony should be the goal instead of one spouse winning the giving discussion.

Family backgrounds impact giving. One spouse may have come from a family where giving was an integral part of life. The parents may have invited missionaries to their home and always met any need that came along. The other spouse may have come from a home where the parents didn't give much to charity, if at all. The key point is to realize that different backgrounds can cause hesitancy on the part of one or both partners.

This is what happened in my marriage. Early on Julie and I didn't give much because I hadn't seen giving modeled in my family while I was growing up. Although Julie wanted to give and came from a family that gave freely, she didn't push me to give. Rather, she let me grow spiritually to where I really wanted to give. And then she allowed me the freedom to develop our family's giving plan—the people and organizations we would support together now that we were married.

What good does it do to give a lot of money to others and to charity and experience disunity and frustration on the home front? Julie and I have found that it's critical to communicate in this area just as we do about investments. Although the issue is giving, that doesn't mean there isn't the potential for conflict. Julie and I have found that it's critical to communicate about *where* we give and *how much* we give.

Conclusion

Giving is thought of as a good thing, and it is if it is done prayerfully and in harmony with your spouse. It's good if it doesn't cause a stumbling block for the recipient (by contributing to slothfulness or enabling poor behavior), for your spouse, for your marriage relationship, or for you. It's good if it's done with the right attitude. Giving is *not* good if it drives a wedge in your marriage. What good does it do if you build the entire education wing on your church and lose your spouse?

As Rob and Sarah discussed their viewpoints on giving and the reasons behind them, they grew closer. Even though Sarah really wanted to give more to the building fund, she understood Rob's concerns and didn't want to push him. She realized he was providing for her and the kids, and she became more appreciative about what they contributed to the general fund at church. That in and of itself had been a big step for Rob. They both agreed to continue to make giving part of their financial discussions and committed to not letting it become a source of conflict.

Game Plan

1. Do you and your spouse agree on your giving amounts?

2. How do you decide where to give?

3. Is one of you more reluctant to give than the other?

4. Have you found that your backgrounds come into play in the giving arena? Explain.

5. What action steps do you need to take to have more harmony in this area?

Chapter 12

A Game Plan for Communication

Rob and Sarah both grabbed a cup of coffee and glanced at their watches. It was only 9:30, and they were excited when they realized they only had one more decision to talk about. They were sure they could get on the road in time to have lunch at the restaurant and take a leisurely drive home.

Decision 8: What Is Our Strategy for Discussing Money?

Rob and Sarah, like many couples, needed to have a game plan as to how they were going to continue to discuss and review the eight major and potentially volatile financial decisions. As we've made our way through these chapters, we've seen that we need to make decisions regarding issues such as debt, who pays the bills, how budget amounts are set, and how investments will be made.

> *Problems related to money may appear to be financial, but they may be nothing more than communication issues.*

It's obvious that a key step in solving the various problems that money can cause in a marriage is to have a game plan to communicate. Couples need a plan not only to communicate about specific money issues but also to discuss their priorities and purposes as a couple. To say, "Honey, I just want you to know that I'm planning on betting our whole paycheck next week on the Super Bowl," is clear communication, but it probably won't promote harmony.

Communication is key because even though the problems related to money may appear to be financial, they may be nothing more than communication issues. Many times I've heard a wife explain, "If he would only talk to me and let me know what's going on, I would be more supportive." And I've often heard a husband say, "She just doesn't understand how hard I work and how difficult it is right now. All she does is spend."

The issue of money is so volatile that many couples "blow up" at each other when they try to discuss it. How can we have productive conversations about money without disrupting marriage harmony? In this chapter we'll look at the motivation, mechanics, and means of good communication.

Motivation for Communication

Motivation is "that which inspires people to action and encourages them to follow through to completion." What motivates husbands and wives to communicate? We will only communicate effectively and consistently if we understand and hold in high esteem the marriage relationship. We must be committed to it. So, if you value your marriage highly, you'll do what it takes to develop good communication skills and not allow money issues to disrupt your unity.

In our world today, this motivation to communicate comes most clearly from a solid understanding of God's Word. To set a solid foundation, let's focus on a few verses from the Amplified Bible (note: text inside brackets is part of the Amplified Version's paraphrase).

In 1 Corinthians 1:10 Paul writes:

> I urge and entreat you, brethren, by the name of our Lord Jesus Christ, that all of you be in perfect harmony and full agreement in what you say, and that there be no dissensions or factions or divisions among you, but that you be perfectly united in your common understanding and in your opinions and judgments.

Our motivation for communication, whether about finances or any other area, should be to create harmony and agreement. Ephesians 4:29 admonishes:

> Let no foul or polluting language, nor evil word nor unwholesome or worthless talk [ever] come out of your mouth, but only such [speech] as is good and beneficial to the spiritual progress of others, as is fitting to the need and the occasion, that it may be a blessing and give grace (God's favor) to those who hear it.

Philippians 2:2 adds:

> Fill up and complete my joy by living in harmony and being of the same mind and one in purpose, having the same love, being in full accord and of one harmonious mind and intention.

First Peter 3:8-9 says:

> All [of you] should be of one and the same mind (united in spirit), sympathizing [with one another], loving [each other] as brethren [of one household], compassionate and courteous (tenderhearted and humble). Never return evil for evil or insult for insult (scolding, tongue-lashing, berating), but on the contrary blessing [praying for their welfare, happiness, and protection, and truly pitying and loving them]. For know that to this you have been called, that you may yourselves inherit a blessing [from God—that you may obtain a blessing as heirs, bringing welfare and happiness and protection].

It's clear that the God of the universe desires that we live harmoniously and be of one mind. This should be our motivation for communicating! We need to purpose in our hearts to cooperate and not let a temporal tool such as money disrupt or ruin our God-ordained relationships—our marriages.

The system to handle conflict that follows is one Julie and I developed when we were engaged, and it has worked well for us for more than 30 years of marriage. We implemented it because we are both choleric personalities and her dad told us, "You will destroy each other if you don't have a plan to handle conflict." So we decided we'd better do so. We hope you find some truths and insights from our plan that will work for you and your spouse as well.

Let's begin with a look at what the New American Standard Bible says about marriage and communication. Read these passages thoughtfully.

- "Then the LORD God said, 'It is not good for the man to be alone; I will make him a helper suitable for him'" (Genesis 2:18).

- "The LORD God caused a deep sleep to fall upon the man, and he slept; then He took one of his ribs and closed up the flesh at that place. The LORD God fashioned into a woman the rib which He had taken from the man, and brought her to the man. The man said, 'This is now bone of my bones, and flesh of my flesh; she shall be called Woman, because she was taken out of Man.' For this reason a man shall leave his father and his mother, and be joined to his wife; and they shall become one flesh" (2:21-24).

- "O magnify the LORD with me, and let us exalt His name together" (Psalm 34:3).

- "How blessed is everyone who fears the LORD, who walks in His ways. When you shall eat of the fruit of your hands, you will be happy and it will be well with you. Your wife shall be like a fruitful vine within your house, your children like olive plants around your table. Behold, for thus shall the man be blessed who fears the LORD" (128:1-4).

- "Let your fountain be blessed, and rejoice in the wife of your youth" (Proverbs 5:18).

- "Better is a dry morsel and quietness with it than a house full of feasting with strife" (17:1).

- "The beginning of strife is like letting out water, so abandon the quarrel before it breaks out" (17:14).

- "Enjoy life with the woman whom you love all the days of your fleeting life which He has given to you under the sun;

for this is your reward in life and in your toil in which you have labored under the sun" (Ecclesiastes 9:9).

- "'For I hate divorce,' says the LORD, the God of Israel, 'and him who covers his garment with wrong,' says the LORD of hosts. 'So take heed to your spirit, that you do not deal treacherously'" (Malachi 2:16).

- "Some Pharisees came to Jesus, testing Him and asking, 'Is it lawful for a man to divorce his wife for any reason at all?' And He answered and said, 'Have you not read that He who created them from the beginning made them male and female, and said, "For this reason a man shall leave his father and mother and be joined to his wife, and the two shall become one flesh." So they are no longer two, but one flesh. What therefore God has joined together, let no man separate.' They said to Him, 'Why then did Moses command to give her a certificate of divorce and send her away?' He said to them, 'Because of your hardness of heart Moses permitted you to divorce your wives; but from the beginning it has not been this way'" (Matthew 19:3-8).

- "Love is patient, love is kind and is not jealous; love does not brag and is not arrogant, does not act unbecomingly; it does not seek its own, is not provoked, does not take into account a wrong suffered, does not rejoice in unrighteousness, but rejoices with the truth; bears all things, believes all things, hopes all things, endures all things" (1 Corinthians 13:4-7).

- "Put them all aside: anger, wrath, malice, slander, and abusive speech from your mouth. Do not lie to one another, since you laid aside the old self with its evil practices" (Colossians 3:8-9).

- "Let your speech always be with grace, as though seasoned with salt, so that you will know how you should respond to each person" (4:6).

- "[An overseer] must be one who manages his own household well, keeping his children under control with all dignity (but if a man does not know how to manage his own household, how will he take care of the church of God?)" (1 Timothy 3:4-5).

- "[Appoint elders...] namely, if any man is above reproach, the husband of one wife, having children who believe, not accused of dissipation or rebellion" (Titus 1:6).

- "Everyone must be quick to hear, slow to speak and slow to anger; for the anger of man does not achieve the righteousness of God" (James 1:19-20).

This system has four basic ground rules:

- Don't raise your voice (Ephesians 4:31-32).
- Don't egg your spouse on or be antagonistic (1 Peter 3:9).
- Don't make derogatory remarks (Ephesians 4:29; Colossians 3:8-9).
- Deal with the problem before the sun goes down (Ephesians 4:26).

We'll discuss these ground rules in more detail by discovering the mechanics of good communication.

The Mechanics of Communication

As you read through this section, please refer to chart 12.1, "Communication Flowchart" on the next page.

The first step to establishing good communication is to take the time to become a student of your spouse. You want to understand how he or she responds to frustrating circumstances and conflicts. Each of us has a certain set of "indicators" or "signs" we exhibit when we're frustrated or upset about something. Understanding temperaments and differences will help us be more perceptive of these indicators. For instance, when Julie becomes upset, her indicators are that she becomes quieter and loses her sense of humor. When I'm upset, I usually respond by changing the subject or talking about side issues. When either one of

Communication Flowchart

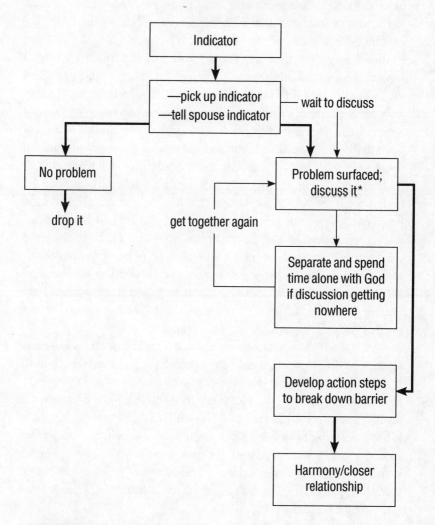

*Ground Rules
- Don't raise voices (Eph. 4:31-32).
- Don't egg the other person on (1 Pet. 3:9).
- Don't make derogatory remarks (Eph. 4:29; Col. 3:8-9).
- Deal with it before the sun goes down (Eph. 4:26).

Chart 12.1

us exhibits these indicators, Julie and I know we need to take the time to communicate about what is bothering one or both of us.

Once the indicators have surfaced, it's important to be sensitive to them. Too often they are ignored (often by the husband), which can lead to greater conflict later. There are two ways to show sensitivity. First, you respond to the indicator you see in your spouse's behavior with a question such as "Is anything bothering you?" or "What's wrong?" This shows you've picked up on a signal something is amiss and want to discuss it. Second, if you're upset and your spouse isn't picking up on your indicators, then it's your responsibility to tell him or her.

If I'm not being sensitive and picking up on Julie's frustration, she needs to tell me something's bothering her. As you can see from the flowchart, one of our ground rules is that any problem must be discussed before the sun goes down (Ephesians 4:26). This helps us avoid greater problems that can occur when small frustrations aren't dealt with speedily. The primary point is that the issue must be discussed before bedtime. I know many husbands may find this especially hard because we men don't tend to talk much. Establishing a time limit of bedtime helps us get around our reluctance.

Once the indicator has been brought into the open and there is agreement that a problem needs to be resolved, you can talk about it. In many cases it's so easy for one spouse to ask, "Is anything wrong?" and the other one will say, "No, everything is fine," when the answer is really, "Yes, something's wrong." "Yes" tends to be our normal response to "Is everything okay?" It takes a sensitive, consistent, and perceptive spouse to continue to prod until the frustration or issue is brought out. If you know (have taken the time to find out) your spouse's indicators, you'll know when there could be a problem, so you won't be easily sidetracked by an initial denial.

Let me illustrate this way. Say a husband comes home from a tough day at the office. Unbeknown to him, his wife has had trouble balancing the checkbook, and there appears to be an overdraft. She's not in a very good mood. He picks up on this when he walks into the house. He asks her if anything is wrong. She says, "No. Well, it's nothing really."

> *The keys to effective communication are to take the time, be persistent, talk out the problem, and pray together.*

The husband accepts this "no" and goes about his business, although he wonders why she's in such a foul mood. Let me assure you that it's much better for him to take the time to draw her out and discover what's going on. This allows her to express her frustrations and opens up the opportunity to deal with the situation. And the same thing works when the husband is frustrated and the wife notices.

Note that the situation doesn't have to be dealt with immediately. Sometimes it's appropriate to wait to discuss the problem. If I'm at a party and I notice that Julie is upset about something, that's probably not the best time to have a heavy discussion. It's better to wait until we're in private. Given the ground rule that frustrations must be discussed before the sun goes down, it's important that we communicate as soon as possible (you don't want to be up all night dealing with a problem).

Here is where the other three ground rules come in. And yes, they're not always easy!

- Don't raise your voice.
- Don't egg the other person on.
- Don't make derogatory remarks.

Many times when I've noticed my wife is frustrated and I've asked about it, my first thought in responding to her answer is to say something like "That's the stupidest thing I've ever heard!" That kind of remark antagonizes my spouse, disrupts the harmony in our relationship, and breaks down the communication even more. If the discussion is to go forward to resolution and emotions are high, I recommend separating for a set amount of time (no longer than one hour). During this time to cool off, each of you needs to spend time alone with God, praying as David did:

Search me, O God, and know my heart;
Try me and know my anxious thoughts;
And see if there be any hurtful way in me;
And lead me in the everlasting way (Psalm 139:23-24).

During this time of separation you may often discover that the dispute is your problem as much as it is your spouse's problem. Then get together to discuss the problem.

The keys to effective communication are take the time, be persistent, talk out the problem, and pray together. It's worth the effort! Julie and I have been up several nights very late working through a problem, but it's such a joy to know the problem has been resolved before we go to bed. Over the years we've found that when conflicts are worked through and resolved, they become stepping-stones to a stronger marriage. As I noted earlier, if problems are allowed to fester and grow day after day, the unity of the marriage is disrupted.

As you and your spouse discuss the problem, determine some specific action steps that will solve it. In the area of finances, for example, many frustrating problems are caused when there is no cash-flow control system. A specific action step to promote harmony would be to set up a budget and—with the input of both spouses—assign specific areas of responsibility. If investments are the frustration point, perhaps a commitment to communicate options before any final decisions are made would be a good action step.

Hopefully as you've read this book, you've also learned more about why your spouse responds the way he or she does to some financial situations. Also, you may have discovered some appropriate steps you can take to promote harmony and avoid conflict in your marriage. My prayer is that you and your mate will experience fewer and fewer negative discussions or fights about money by developing a good financial plan.

Two More Important Guidelines

The bottom-line goal in communicating is to establish a closer and more harmonious relationship. To that end, let's take a look at two more important guidelines.

Don't settle for a stalemate. It's not healthy for a couple to leave a financial issue unresolved or for a husband and wife to remain on opposite sides of a dispute about money. Some people say that it's okay to agree to disagree, but how much harmony can result from that?

I propose that couples should never allow a stalemate on an important issue. The purpose of good communication is to let each spouse clearly state his or her position on an issue. Once this is done, if there is an impasse or disagreement regarding the best answer or action, the husband has the final say (1 Corinthians 11:3). Remember, God has given the husband the responsibility to make the decisions in his family—not because he's smarter or better than his wife, but because God knew someone had to be the final decision maker. Although the wife may not feel it or realize it at the time, not having to carry the weight of "big" decisions is a blessing.

> *How your spouse and you handle the decision-making process is far more important than the actual outcome.*

Husbands, your position is not to be taken lightly. You should take great care to make sure you get your wife's input and weigh it carefully before making any decision, especially a decision that directly opposes your wife's desire. You may need to resist the urge to say "I told you so" to your wife if the decision you make works out.

Wives, you may need to exercise faith and trust God for the decision your husbands make, especially if it isn't what you believe is the best choice. It's his responsibility to make the decision. Your responsibility is to submit to that decision and trust God for the outcome that aligns with His will. You may need to resist the urge to say "I told you so" if your husband's decision doesn't work out.

Remember, money is a tool, nothing more. How your spouse and you handle the decision-making process is far more important than the actual outcome.

Julie and I have had several occasions in our married life to test this process for avoiding stalemates. It really does work. If we're faced with a decision that we don't totally agree on, I listen to Julie's input and weigh it carefully before making the final decision. Julie always follows giving her input with these words: "That is my input. Now I'm trusting

God to work with you to make the best decision. I'm with you no matter what you decide." With those words she gives me the freedom to make the decision but also encourages me to spend time with God to gain His wisdom. Plus, I typically go back and make sure I've really listened to Julie's input. I've learned over the years that her counsel is right more often than not.

This brings us to the second very important guideline.

Never take revenge. Peter tells us to not repay evil for evil but, instead, to give a blessing (1 Peter 3:8-9). Therefore, if the husband makes a decision the wife is not comfortable with (a bad investment, for instance), she might frivolously spend money just to get even with him. Or he might take revenge on her by not telling her the next time he does something in the investment arena. Neither of these responses will promote unity in the marriage. Harmony is much more important than money.

Setting Up Your Own Planning Weekend

One of the practical ways we've found to facilitate communication in our marriage relationship is to have a planning weekend regularly, just like Rob and Sarah did. This is simply a weekend set aside for us as husband and wife to get away by ourselves for the purpose of communicating and taking inventory of our relationship. During this weekend we discuss finances, children, work, goals, and dreams.

Here is a format for the weekend we've found helpful. Although this doesn't have to be adhered to, it illustrates the important balance between work and play.

Financial Planning Weekend

Topics: Finances, children, spiritual life, social life, work, goals, major decisions, dreams

Friday: 2:00 to 4:00 Arrive at destination
4:00 to 6:00 Rest and unwind
6:00 Dinner and discuss a topic

Saturday: 8:00 to 10:00 Breakfast and time alone with God
10:00-12:00 Discuss a topic or continue discussion of previous topic

12:00-5:00 Lunch, shop, recreation
6:00 Dinner and discuss a topic

Sunday: 8:00 to 10:00 Breakfast and time alone with God
10:00 to 12:00 Discuss action steps to promote and
enhance marriage

Caution: When you go on a planning weekend, expect to do some work and come away with one or two specific action steps that will enhance your relationship. Usually both spouses have been busy with the children or a job so when they get away for the weekend, they see it as a great opportunity to relax, watch football games, and shop—anything except plan. Setting an agenda beforehand and committing to discussing the desired goals will help make the weekend a success.

In some cases, if you bring to the surface a very strategic issue that must be discussed at length, you may decide to stay on that issue for the entire weekend. The important result is that you accomplish one or two specific things that will make your relationship better as a result of the weekend.

To illustrate what can happen if expectations aren't adjusted *before* the planning weekend, let me share a story that happened to Julie and me. We'd scheduled a planning weekend several weeks in advance, and I was looking forward to our time together to talk over some key issues in handling our finances and raising the kids. Being the planning type, I saw no reason to wait until we arrived at our destination to begin discussing the topics I knew we wanted to cover. We hadn't driven more than 25 minutes into a 2-hour drive when I asked Julie some planning questions to get her input.

She didn't respond with much enthusiasm, and after a short time, she said, "I can't believe it! We just left home, and you're already wanting to plan and be organized. You haven't even given me a chance to unwind. I've been with the kids all day, and you want to start planning before we even get a chance to relax and get where we're going?"

That was when we realized that a planning weekend can only be a success if both husband and wife have the right expectations about it. It's neither a weekend of fun and games nor a weekend of intense, unrelenting work. You can do your marriage more harm than good if you don't agree on a reasonable balance. Julie and I soon overcame our timing problem, and we had a very productive weekend.

Discussion Starter

Chart 12.2, "Marital Intimacy Checklist," at the end of this chapter is a practical tool that can be a good way to start the communication process at the outset of your planning weekend. Julie and I typically answer each of the questions individually, and then we get together and compare our responses. If we have a major difference in how we perceive our unity in any area, that is where we start the discussion.

Take financial intimacy, for example. If Julie has put a 1 and I have put down a 5, obviously we are perceiving our finances dramatically differently, which means there is a tremendous potential for conflict. If we have basically the same numbers in an area, we don't focus on it as much as other areas during this particular weekend.

The Means of Communication

If communicating along these guidelines seems impossible, then you need to know that it is impossible! Without walking closely with God and asking the Holy Spirit for wisdom and insight, it's impossible to be truly sensitive to your spouse and tune in to his or her concerns and feelings. By nature humans are selfish. We want our own way. Therefore we need to ask God to give us His wisdom and the sensitivity we need to communicate properly.

Conclusion

As we've learned throughout these pages, money is simply a tool, but our marriages have eternal significance. We've also learned of our need to be sensitive to each other to build harmony into our marriages, and that it's impossible to be sensitive without experiencing the power source of the Holy Spirit as a reality in our lives.

It's my prayer that before you close this book you will deal seriously with the God of the universe from whom the power for a harmonious marriage flows. May God bless you and allow you to experience an abundant, fruitful, and harmonious marriage.

And now, let's have a final visit with Rob and Sarah as they prepare to implement all they've learned.

As Rob and Sarah packed their bags for the trip home they glanced at the clock. Eleven on the nose. *Great!* That would give them enough time to stop at the cafe they had passed and still be home by five o'clock, when the grandparents were expecting them. They stopped to say goodbye to John and Dottie before heading out. They both realized that the notebook John and Dottie had created for them to go through had been very eye opening and helpful. They both agreed it had been a life-changing weekend.

"John and Dottie," Rob said, as he shook hands with John, "thanks for a great weekend. Sarah and I had a very productive time."

"We're so glad," John said. "That's always our goal for couples."

"How did you know to have so many questions on money in the notebook?" Sarah asked.

"Well, that's really quite simple to answer," Dottie said. "Through all the years together, we've found that money tends to create the most conflict in marriages. That was true of ours. If couples can learn to communicate about money, they can communicate about anything."

"I think you're right about that," agreed Rob. "We sure learned a lot about ourselves this weekend, and we know it will help us in our marriage. We can't wait to tell our friends about this place."

"That's great," said John. "We appreciate it. Have a safe trip."

They said their goodbyes, and Rob and Sarah got into their vehicle. As they rolled out of the gravel drive of Village Crest Inn, Rob couldn't help but think about what a great weekend it had been to reflect on his life and his marriage. He realized he needed to keep a better balance in his life by living according to time priorities rather than income priorities. He knew success wasn't measured by his income. He was now more committed to communicating with Sarah in the money area and encouraging her in her role of helper, companion, and nurturer. He had probably underestimated how difficult her job was in raising their posterity. He knew it wouldn't come easy to communicate better once he hit the office doors on Monday morning, but as a starting point, he was going to write on his calendar a date night each Sunday. He realized he needed Sarah's wise insights about how they handled their money and set their budget. He really did love the woman sitting next to him!

"Hey, honey, here is the Blow-Me-Down Covered Bridge again…"

"I know you want to stop. No problem. We have time," Rob responded, surprising Sarah.

Several minutes later they got back into the car and continued toward the cafe. Sarah couldn't help but think about the change in Rob over the past 48 hours. The fact that he really didn't mind stopping at the bridge was more evidence. She'd thought long and hard about their discussion on income and investments and debt and realized better how Rob viewed those issues. That had been a real eye opener. She realized she needed to be more content and affirm him and make sure they lived within his income. She didn't want him to feel any pressure from her to make more money. She also realized that getting a job wouldn't be best for the family right now. The kids needed her at home, and Rob did too. She was committed to being a helper to that man sitting next to her! She smiled as she thought about how much she really loved him.

Friends, how about you? Do you remember the day you were married? You were so much in love. You promised to stay together "until death us do part." Then life kind of happened and communication waned. The kids and dog came along, and the bills piled up. It's not too late to take action to make your marriage stronger. Study and apply the principles found in God's Word, and a harmonious marriage is possible and waiting for you.

May God bless you as you make money a nonissue in your marriage. I pray that you will experience the joy and fulfillment He intends for you.

Game Plan

1. Have you ever attended or held a planning weekend? If

yes, would you do it again? Why not schedule a planning weekend right now?

2. Discuss as a couple how you would structure the weekend. How long it would be, where you would go, what you would want to accomplish—such as budgeting issues, children issues, upcoming vacations, family goals and dreams.

3. Discuss what you'd need to do to prepare for a planning weekend: get babysitters, make reservations, save the money. Then write down action steps to accomplish these tasks.

Marital Intimacy Checklist

As you review your marriage, how would you evaluate *your* degree of satisfaction with the following items? Circle the number which best describes your feelings.

	Very Dissatisfied	Somewhat Dissatisfied	Neutral	Somewhat Satisfied	Very Satisfied
1. **Spiritual Intimacy** *(oneness before God)*	1	2	3	4	5
2. **Work Intimacy** *(sharing common tasks)*	1	2	3	4	5
3. **Intellectual Intimacy** *(closeness in ideas)*	1	2	3	4	5
4. **Recreational Intimacy** *(relating in fun and play)*	1	2	3	4	5
5. **Emotional Intimacy** *(being on same wavelength)*	1	2	3	4	5
6. **Crisis Intimacy** *(closeness in problems and pain)*	1	2	3	4	5
7. **Conflict Intimacy** *(understanding in facing and struggling with differences)*	1	2	3	4	5
8. **Creative Intimacy** *(sharing in acts of creating together)*	1	2	3	4	5
9. **Commitment Intimacy** *(common benefits from shared efforts)*	1	2	3	4	5
10. **Aesthetic Intimacy** *(sharing experiences of beauty)*	1	2	3	4	5
11. **Sexual Intimacy**	1	2	3	4	5
12. **Communication Intimacy** *(feeling of openness in every area)*	1	2	3	4	5
13. **Financial Intimacy** *(communication on finances)*	1	2	3	4	5

After each spouse responds separately, get together and discuss why you responded the way you did.

Chart 12.2

Reproduced by permission of Ronald Blue & Co., Atlanta, GA

Chapter 13

A Woman's Perspective on Her God-Given Roles

by Julie Crosson

When I began my career as a nurse anesthetist, I had no use for a husband. My dreams didn't include marriage, kids, cooking, cleaning, and a husband to whom I would have to submit—especially one who didn't make much money. No, *I* was going to make a lot of money and enjoy my freedom. I wanted it all: sports cars, travel, clothes, a high-end job, and an exciting life.

I came from a very godly home where my mom and dad loved each other very much. My mom was an incredible example of biblical submission, so you would think I would have been looking for that kind of marriage. I wasn't.

Then I met Russ. After we dated for a year, Russ asked me to marry him. I told him no! The truth was that I didn't want to have to submit. And along with the issue of submission came the fact that Russ was a high school math teacher, and I was determined not to be poor.

I became very confused. I couldn't sleep at night. The Bible says God isn't the author of confusion, so it became clear to me that sin was clouding my ability to think. I asked the Lord to reveal the sin in my life. Immediately selfishness, pride, and not trusting God and His Word paraded across my mind. I wrongly thought the things money could buy would make me happy, and I was unwilling to do without them. As I confessed my unbelief and unwillingness to trust God, I was able to think clearly again. It dawned on me that Russ had all the qualities I could ever want in a husband: a deep ability to love me, strong character, and a vibrant walk with God.

That night I decided I would trust God. I then made a commitment to Russ for the rest of my life, no matter what that meant. I was willing to submit, live on a teacher's income, live in Africa, and watch football on Sunday afternoons if that's what it took. I would be obedient to *God's plan* for marriage.

Once I made that decision, I knew I needed to renew my mind. I started studying the Bible's guidelines for a wife's role in marriage. I began to see that understanding my role would directly affect how I handled and responded to money issues within my marriage.

Discovering My Job Description as "Helper"

To begin studying my role as a wife, I started at the beginning. I went to Genesis 2:18: "The LORD God said, 'It is not good for the man to be alone; I will make him a helper suitable for him.'" The one word that defines my existence as a married woman is "*helper*." I went to the dictionary to understand "help." I personalized each definition of help:

> *I am to make it easier for Russ to exist, develop, happen, improve.* This could mean moving to another city for a better job for him or taking the pressure off him for more money.
>
> *I am to cause improvement in Russ.* This could include helping him feel he is a success by pointing out what he does well and making him happier with himself, me, and his job.
>
> *I am to give assistance, be cooperative, useful, beneficial to Russ.* This could be by being in harmony with his goals and dreams and studying his career so I better understand his world.
>
> *I will supply what I can to help Russ accomplish his ends or relieve his wants.* This could include asking him what would help him most—providing home-cooked meals, creating a home he feels comfortable in, ensuring peace at home.

The antonym of the word "help" is "hinder": "to get in the way of, make difficult for, obstruct." "To obstruct" means "to retard progress by placing obstacles in the way."

> *I could hinder Russ by restraining him.* This might include refusing to relocate or to live on less money. After we'd been married a year, Russ felt God was calling him to go into financial planning. I wanted to move to Phoenix where my family was, but Russ said he needed to go to the best place to learn financial planning—Atlanta. I agreed to move with him. Not moving when God was leading my husband to Atlanta would be telling God I had a better plan for our future. That would be a dangerous situation to be in.
>
> *I could hinder Russ by getting in his way.* This might include complaining about everything or making him feel what he provides isn't good enough. By getting in his way, I might contribute to him becoming worried at work and not being able to focus.
>
> *I could hinder Russ by frustrating him.* I might do this by buying things he doesn't agree with and adding to the debt load.
>
> *I could hinder Russ by slowing his progress.* I might do this by wanting him to come home early to help me with my job (homemaking and raising the children). This might cause him to be unable to concentrate 100 percent at work or feel he can't stay late if he needs to.

After studying the wife's role of "helper," I wanted to explore what characteristics a godly wife should have or develop.

Discovering the Qualities of a Godly Wife

The next assignment I set for myself was to check out what Scripture taught about the character qualities of a godly wife. I went to Proverbs 31.

Trustworthy

The first passage that gave me insight was "the heart of her husband trusts in her confidently...so that he has no lack of [honest] gain or need of [dishonest] spoil" (Proverbs 31:11 AMP, brackets in original). Lack of honest gain could be overspending or wasting our income. Need of dishonest spoil could be making Russ feel he doesn't earn enough to provide for our family.

Any comment or "I wish" statement could cause him to believe I'm not happy with what I have or with what he provides. That might contribute to him feeling like a failure, thus pressuring him to cheat on his income taxes or jump into a get-rich-quick scheme.

I asked a group of young moms to ask their husbands what put them under pressure. All of the husbands agreed that it was when their wives said, "I wish…"

> *I decided before the Lord that Russ would always be able to trust me in the area of finances.*

Matthew Henry's Commentary says, "[A wife] contributes so much to [a husband's] content that he shall have no need of spoil; he thinks himself so happy in her that he envies not those who have most of the wealth of this world; he needs it not, he has enough, having such a wife."[1] George Santa, in his book *A Modern Study in the Book of Proverbs,* wrote: "Everything is so carefully and economically managed [by her], he is never tempted to dishonesty to fulfill his desires, no need to leave his happy home. Her husband's comfort is her interest and her rest. To live for him is her highest happiness."[2]

Overall, that means my husband needs to trust me. So I needed to decide which is more important: securing my husband's trust or buying what I want and always having conflict over finances. Proverbs 31:12 says: "[His wife] does him good and not evil all the days of her life." I made this my personal verse in regard to my marriage to Russ. While we were engaged, Russ told me of his concern about our future joint account and especially adding my name to his credit card account. It didn't help his comfort level that I had never balanced a checkbook. I did record everything; I just didn't do the math part. Russ was worried about my ability to live within a budget.

I decided before the Lord that Russ would always be able to trust me in the area of finances. Too much was at stake. As a result, I became very serious about how I spent money. We agreed to talk to each other about any unplanned purchase over $20. I knew Russ didn't like surprises, and my marriage was way more important than issues about money. I decided to look at living within the budget as a game. Looking for sales and bargains became fun. Seeing what I could do within the monthly budget was a 30-day challenge that happened every month. I enjoyed beating the system!

Russ learned that he could trust my heart. He discovered that I was for him and happy to help him reach his financial goals. We have now come full circle to the point that Russ insists I buy things for the house. He sometimes tells me that *I have to go shopping* for clothes!

Adaptive

First Peter 3:1 says, "Wives, be submissive to your own husbands." The Living Bible paraphrases this, "Wives, fit in with your husbands' plans." The Amplified Version says, "You married women, be submissive to your own husbands [...adapt yourselves to them]" (brackets in original). "Adapt" means "to make to fit; to knit together; be properly adjusted to the shape intended." To me, the words "adjust," "adapt," and "fit," mean—in a financial sense—to adapt to his income and the lifestyle we've agreed is the best for our family. I fit in with Russ's plans and adjust my life to his by wrapping my life around him. Everything I do with money has an eye to being knit together with him.

Submissive

"Submission" is a military term meaning "to stay under the authority of." I understand and appreciate the protection the authority structure affords our military. I've enjoyed looking for societal relationships that demonstrate submission: vice-president (to president), assistant coach (to coach), copilot (to pilot), and vice-principal (to principal), to name a few.

Why is it when I encounter these authorities in various situations I have no problem following what they say or advocate, but when it comes to submitting to my own husband not only am I resistant but today's culture considers the idea that I submit to Russ degrading?

There is another aspect of submission I saw because I worked with my physician dad. The nurses who worked for him were unhappy over pay issues, and he became less and less willing to work things out with them. It dawned on me that I never saw this attitude in him at home. My mom's joyful submission to Dad allowed him to feel good about his life and his home. He didn't have to fight for his rightful place, and it made a difference in how he was viewed by and interacted with other people. He was highly respected as a Bible teacher and a leader in the community. The nurses' lack of submission brought out the worst in him and made it difficult for everyone to come to an agreement. (This doesn't excuse the fact that Dad's heart wasn't right toward them, but it does point out how to best help a husband.)

One of the hardest questions I've ever been asked over the years is, "What do I do if my husband is making bad financial decisions? Do I submit and let him wreck the train?" There is no easy answer, but I believe a wife should give input if the husband is willing to listen and then she must trust God with the outcome. The choice seems to be between taking over and defying the husband or letting him learn the hard way and loving him regardless of his bad decisions. If these families get back on their feet financially in five years, will the husband be grateful for how his wife encouraged and went through it with him or will his wife have been a burden and hindrance to him through the struggle?

I've made it a point never to say "I told you so" to Russ. All that does is drive a wedge between us, and I always want us to grow closer as a team. So when I question the route Russ chooses to go after we've discussed the situation together, I talk to the Lord about it. I ask Him to intervene and protect us. Then I encourage Russ as honestly as I can. It's very important for him to hear what I think.

I've found that it's very effective to tell Russ, "Honey, here's my input. Now I'm trusting God with your decision." I've been amazed at how powerful my position of *influence* has been when my attitude reflects the desire to support my husband and stay under his authority. In fact, being in submission to Russ has saved me from making some really bad financial mistakes. And his leadership has taken the pressure off me when it comes to weighty decisions.

Are there limits to submission? The answer is yes. For instance, God will not absolve me from responsibility if Russ asks me to do something against God's principles and I go ahead and do it. Submission isn't an excuse for sin. If my husband abuses his position of leadership and asks me to go against a moral law of Scripture, I submit to the higher authority of God. At this point, a third party such as a pastor or counselor may be needed. First Peter 3:1-2 reads, "Be submissive to your own husbands so that even if any of them are disobedient to the word, they may be won without a word by the behavior of their wives, as they observe your chaste and respectful behavior." This seems clear that if our husbands are not where they should be spiritually (or where we think they should be), our responses to them are important to God.

Content

Over the years I've found that one of the greatest things I can do for Russ is to be content. I'm reminded of the story of two little boys who were given shovels and pointed to a room full of manure. One boy grumbled the whole time he was digging. The other went to work very excited. The reason? He figured that with all that manure, there had to be a pony in there somewhere!

One day I was complaining to myself about all the laundry, cleaning, cooking, ironing, and other "thankless" jobs I had to do. I took a break and picked up my Bible. I ran across Proverbs 14:4: "Where no oxen are, the manger is clean." My perspective was instantly changed. All my work meant I was blessed with a husband and children!

Contentment is an attitude. It's realizing God has provided everything I need for my present circumstances. Contentment is having a mind at peace because I'm satisfied with what I have and my circumstances. Dr. Sam Peoples has a saying that helps me: "The circumstances of life and the people around me in life do not make me the way I am but reveal the way I am."[3] Is how I'm responding to my circumstances revealing a heart of contentment? I ask this question often. Contentment is a spiritual issue, so I looked up what God says about it.

First Timothy 6:8 says, "If we have food and covering, with these we shall be content." I have food and clothing, so am I content? Yes. I do realize that being content with what I have seems almost tragic since our culture encourages us to strive for more of everything. Luke 3:14 says, "Be content with your wages." That's not hard to interpret. Hebrews 13:5 says, "Make sure your character is free from the love of money, being content with what you have; for He Himself has said, 'I will never desert you, nor will I ever forsake you.'" In Philippians 4:11-13, Paul wrote that he had learned to be content in all circumstances. Even our traditional marriage vows address the money issue. When I married Russ, I vowed before God and the people present to love, cherish, honor, and obey him, for richer or for poorer. That meant I committed to being content with his income for the rest of my life. A vow is a very serious thing to God.

There is a connection between finances and contentment.
The key is thankfulness.

One way for me to learn contentment is to live frugally. This takes financial pressure off Russ right from the start. Then he can choose to add expenses as he's comfortable with his work and our lifestyle. Another way to be content is to wait patiently until we can pay cash for an item. When we bought our first house, we decided to wait until we'd saved enough money to purchase the dining room table we both really liked. We had to save for two years to be able to pay cash for it. As a result, we appreciate the table so much more.

I ran across a slogan that was used during World War II. This should be a standard feature on every credit card: "Use it up, wear it out, make it do, or do without." There are many benefits of doing without. My mom calls it having a "do without" mindset. I saw firsthand the freedom and joy my dad experienced because my mom didn't pressure him about finances. Another potential problem with using credit cards is that we're not giving God a chance to take care of our needs. Our impatience many times keeps us from seeing His hand in our lives. Paul said, "My God will supply all your needs according to His riches in glory in Christ Jesus" (Philippians 4:19). I've seen two problems with the word "need": a lack of definition and a lack of honesty. Something we "need" is necessary to subsistence. I like to compare "need" with "want" and "desire" to help me use the word correctly. Here's an example of how it helps.

Need	Want	Desire
Bicycle	Car	Luxury Car
Apartment	House	Mansion
Thrift shop clothes	Dept. store brands	Designer labels
Water	Bottled water	Natural spring water

Now, it's important to look at needs and wants with honesty. I have what I *need*. (Most people in the United States have or have access to the essentials.) I even have most of my wants. But I don't have all my desires. And like most people, when I want something I often use the word "need" when technically it's not accurate. For instance, I've told Russ that I *need* new shoes. That isn't right. I already have what I need and even what I want. But now I *desire* new shoes.

For me, there is a connection between finances and contentment. That key is thankfulness. When I'm feeling dissatisfied, I find it helps me to make lists of things I'm grateful for. I also make lists of things I wouldn't take any amount of money for, including my children; my salvation; a husband who loves God and me with a pure heart; my husband having a job he loves; having a mind that works; my sense of humor; the abilities to see, hear, smell, taste, and touch; living in a free country; and having access to competent medical care. You could offer me a million dollars, and I wouldn't give up any of these things. Sometimes I just need to take the time to contemplate all that God has done and thank Him for everything that comes to mind. Reading uplifting books also helps me stay content (see Recommended Resources).

What about the antonym "discontent"? What does "discontent" look like? It means having a disquieted mind, dissatisfaction, uneasiness from disappointed wishes or expectations. Ecclesiastes 5:10 says, "He who loves money will not be satisfied with money." If I love money and what it can buy, I will be discontent. This shows up when I catch myself thinking "I wish I had…" or "I wish I didn't have to…"

> *Husbands don't like feeling they aren't providing or doing enough to keep their wives happy.*

Discontent does two things. First, it keeps me from enjoying what I do have. Second, it makes me long for what I don't have. For instance, I have a weakness for wanting new clothes for social functions. Not only do I wish for something new, at those moments I also dislike all the nice things I already have. We need to be satisfied with what we have already. It's not being discontent to want something new—car, carpet, washing machine, or shoes. The problem is to be discontent with the old until we can afford the new. A good measure of dissatisfaction or discontent is consumer debt. Dave Ramsey summed it up nicely this way: "We buy things we don't need with money we don't have in order to impress people we don't even like."[4]

In Matthew 20:15 we read, "Is your eye envious because I am generous?" God can do what He wants with what is His. To check my heart attitude, I ask: "Am I glad that person gets to drive the car I'd like for myself?" Envy is a feeling of discontent and ill will because of another's advantages or possessions.

Covetousness is desiring more than one needs or being greedy. Colossians 3:5 equates it with idolatry: "So kill...all greed and covetousness, for that is idolatry" (AMP). Discontent reveals my unwillingness to trust God for where I am.

A wife's discontent can put a husband under tremendous pressure. This often shows up because the husband becomes unhappy at work. One time Russ came home and said he'd been in a bad mood at work. A warning flag went up in my mind. I asked if I had done anything recently that he didn't like. He told me I'd made several remarks about how I didn't like living in Atlanta, so he felt he'd made me unhappy by moving here. Husbands don't like feeling they aren't providing or doing enough to keep their wives happy.

A friend of mine complained that her husband wouldn't let her quit work. I asked her if she'd ever told him she was willing to be content on his income. Grinning, she told me he wouldn't mind her staying home, but he'd told her she couldn't have the fancy restaurants and vacations that she wanted if she didn't work. Clearly he felt he couldn't provide enough to keep her happy. Since she wanted the extras, he insisted she work.

Conclusion

When I've spoken to groups of women about fitting in with my husband's plans, two related questions always come up: "What about *me*?" and "What about *my* fulfillment?" Well, that's a question I asked as well. And I have an answer.

I realized that life isn't about me. When I looked for my answers to those questions in the Bible, I found 1 Corinthians 6:19-20: "Do you not know that you...are not your own? For you have been bought with a price: therefore glorify God in your body." Paul wrote to the Romans that "not one of us lives for himself; and not one dies for himself; for if we live, we live for the Lord, or if we die, we die for the Lord; therefore whether we live or die, we are the Lord's." In 1 Corinthians 7:34 we find: "[The woman] who is married is concerned about the things of the world, how she may please her husband." In these verses there is no place for "me" and "my."

I decided the question is really: "Am I willing to obey God when it comes to my marriage?" Most societies recognize that there must be an authority structure for people to exist peacefully together. As a Christian woman, getting married committed me even further to not living for myself. Instead my focus is on God, my husband, and my children.

Russ and I decided before *we got married that I would stay home once children came.* I considered going back to work part-time after they were all in school, but I only have so much emotional energy, so Russ and I agreed that it was best for the family for me to continue to stay home. I'm convinced that God doesn't hold me responsible to help my husband afford a larger house, a nicer car, and more expensive clothes. God will ask me how I did on His job description for me. Did I help Russ and ease his load? Did I stay under his authority? Did I look after my household well?

Unfortunately, sometimes the pressure for a mother of young children to stay in a career outside the home may come from her dad. A letter my dad wrote to me when I quit work set me free from feeling that he would be disappointed if I were a full-time wife, mother, and homemaker. It encouraged me to recognize God's job description for me. Here is a portion of it:

Now then—work. I have some thoughts to submit for your perusal. Namely, I think it is very good for you not to work! In my opinion, you were right on to go ahead and get the training and do the job—and you did it extremely well. But now you are married. That changes things. The anesthesia thing is completely separate from Russ—and you spend most of your waking life in it. [Dad was an anesthesiologist, and I was a nurse anesthetist for his group.] Whereas if you don't work you will spend most of your time being a wife, being involved in Russ's life. That's much better! Anyway, it just this week dawned on me that I hope you don't go back to work. How about that! Rather, you

can be full-time wife and homemaker, which is a real and godly calling and very, very wonderful. You will have plenty to do by being available to people and to Russ.

So when it comes to my marriage and family, basically I ask the Lord
to give me the wisdom to communicate the right things to Russ. I tell
him that I want to help him accomplish his goals so he will feel he is
a success in God's eyes. I want him to be free to do his job well knowing that I'm behind him 100 percent. I want him to know that there's
no pressure from me for more money. I'm willing to stay on the budget we agree on and do whatever it takes to live within our means. I try
not to miss any opportunity to build him up. When the economy dips,
I communicate to Russ that I'm okay if the business takes a downturn.
I remind him that I don't have to have our "stuff" to be happy. I often
say "thank you" to him for working so hard and providing for all my
needs. I'm content right where I am, and I tell him I would move and
live anywhere with him.

> *To fulfill my roles in my marriage as God intended,*
> *my heart has to be right with Him.*

And Russ really appreciates my attitude and affirmations because
it frees him to do his job to the best of his ability rather than worrying
about what I might think or do if our financial situation changed and
our budget became tighter. I tell him frequently that I don't need a bigger house, newer car, or the new fashions in clothes. Most of all, I tell
him that I'm wealthy because I have him and our children. I like this
saying: "We're rich—and someday we may even have money."

Before ending this chapter, I want to mention Proverbs 31:16
because it's commonly taken out of context when discussing a wife's
contribution to the household income: "She considers a field and buys
it; from her earnings she plants a vineyard." Some people say the Proverbs 31 woman was a real estate agent, but that's incorrect. She did
not go to an office eight hours a day and buy and sell vineyards. In
her day there weren't grocery stores, so buying a field to plant a vineyard was an extension of managing her home. The Amplified Bible

paraphrases this verse: "She considers a [new] field before she buys or accepts it [expanding prudently and not courting neglect of her present duties by assuming other duties]" (brackets in original). The Proverbs 31 woman's core responsibility was her home and family. Verse 27 says, "She looks well to how things go in her household" (AMP). Anything outside her home was added only if it didn't interfere with her present duties.

To fulfill my roles in my marriage as God intended, my heart has to be right with Him. I have to let the Holy Spirit control my thoughts, my actions, and my words moment by moment. I like Major Ian Thomas's description of walking in the Spirit: "The One who calls you to a life of righteousness is the One who, by your consent, lives that life of righteousness through you!"[5] He also wrote, "It is only the Spirit of God acting within you who can ever enable you to behave as God intended you to behave!"[6]

To keep my heart and attitude right, I also must be spending time in God's Word. This is the only way I can renew my mind and get God's perspective. In the years I have left, what really matters for eternity is my marriage, my children, and the people around me because people go to heaven—our stuff doesn't

Finances have become a minor part of our marriage. We enjoy reviewing our financial plans and goals because we do it together as a team. We don't fight about where the money goes. At the end of the year when we go over the budget, I thank Russ for providing for us and managing our finances so well. And Russ is pleased with how I handle staying within our budget. He's grateful that I don't put him under financial pressure and that I'm happy to stay on the financial course we have set. We're both grateful that God—through the Holy Spirit and the Bible—is the foundation for our finances. "Now to Him who is able to do exceeding abundantly beyond all that we ask or think, according to the power that works within us ..." (Ephesians 3:20).

Practical Helps

Here are some ways I've found helpful in staying within our budget.

Clothes for Russ and me. We often go shopping together, which reduces impulse purchases. I also have a friend who is a personal shopper, so we shop together too. With her help, I buy half of what I used to and actually wear the clothes I already have.

Children's clothes and toys. I shop neighborhood sales, garage sales, and thrift shops.

Eating out. Most health coaches recommend eating out only once a week. When we do eat out, we don't order drinks because that adds up to 20 percent to the bill! I used to pack bag lunches for Russ and the kids. I also use food and restaurant coupons and specials I find in the newspaper or online.

Gift closet. This has been a huge savings. In a small notebook I keep a list of people I buy gifts for, along with a list of things we've given to each person. When Russ and I sit down to budget, we have a general idea of how many gifts we'll be purchasing and estimate how much we'll spend. We set general limits, such as $30 per Christmas gift, $50 per wedding gift, and so on.

Russ and I also decide ahead of time how much we'll spend on gifts for each other and for our boys on special occasions, such as birthdays and Christmas. Because I have a list of people I buy for, I can purchase gifts all year long and take advantage of sales. This allows us to increase our gift giving. My goal is to be finished with Christmas shopping by the time summer ends. When our boys were little, I didn't shop too far ahead for their gifts because they changed their minds too fast and too often.

I also keep several baby, birthday, graduation, and wedding gifts on hand in my gift storage area—all picked up at sales (after Christmas, end of season, and going out of business).

Controlled shopping. I don't shop a great sale if I don't have the money. Our first Christmas we had zero in the budget for Christmas, so we sent pecans that we cracked and packed by hand. We had no money for a Christmas tree so we cut a branch off a tree in our yard. I would ask God to help you be creative if you have little or no funds in the budget for gifts. Pictures are always welcome yet inexpensive gifts. Letters expressing love for family members are wonderful to give too.

Haircuts. To save money I use coupons for our haircuts. I also checked out a book from our local library and learned how to cut my children's hair. (I encourage you to do this. And if it doesn't turn out well at first, hair always grows out and you can try again.)

Pets. We waited until we had money in savings before getting a pet. Monthly medications, grooming, and veterinary bills need to be factored into your budget for animals. Avoid making impulse decisions about getting a pet and all that goes with it.

Socializing. We invite friends over for meals or desserts. We also meet for yard games, picnics, or popcorn and movies.

A "do without" month. I was inspired to try this by our neighbors. Choose a month and purpose to not spend any money on non-essentials that month.

Cable, internet, and cell phones. The goal is to stay within the budget on these items. Check the bills frequently to see if there are ways to reduce costs. Do without cable for a while. Parents should decide when a child gets a phone. I recommend choosing the cheapest, most basic phone. Costs for pictures, internet, and texting need to be carefully considered. Stay on top of monthly charges.

Papers, magazines, and buying clubs. I make sure that I'm saving money before I sign up. I don't allow automatic renewals so I'll have the opportunity to reevaluate each one every year.

Coupons. I only use coupons or double coupons if I've compared prices and it's an item I typically buy. Check out coupon websites, but remember to stay within the budget even if a "great deal" is offered.

Grocery shopping. I plan weekly menus and do most of my shopping once a week. I take advantage of store sales when planning the menu, and I do use coupons.

Questions to Ask Before Buying

To help us make wise decisions and maintain harmony in our marriage, we ask these questions.

- Is this a need, want, or desire?
- Am I getting the best deal I can for the money?
- Does this purchase honor God and reflect His principles?
- What is my goal with this purchase?

- Will this purchase require extra time for upkeep?
- Will this item hold its value?
- Is this an impulsive or unplanned item? If so, it's best to wait 30 days before making a decision.
- Is getting this item or investing in this part of a get-rich-quick mentality?
- Have I prayed about this purchase?
- Did my husband request this?
- Do my husband and I agree on this purchase?
- Will this purchase put us under financial stress of any kind?
- Is this purchase in our budget?

The Ultimate Power Source

You may have read this entire book and been struck with the realization that you don't have the Power Source within you to enable you to do what's been recommended. You may be sitting there about to finish this book, thinking there were some good ideas shared, but they're basically impossible to implement. If it weren't for my relationship with the Lord God of the universe through His Son Jesus Christ, I wouldn't be able to fulfill my God-given roles, be sensitive to Julie, and experience the joy and harmony we have in our marriage. God, working through the power of the Holy Spirit, enables me to be the best husband possible for my wife.

Just as there are financial principles that are true, there are also spiritual principles that are true. The principles that follow will help you plug into the most potent Power available.

Principle 1: Mankind is separated from God. The Bible teaches that God loves all mankind. He wants everyone to know Him personally. But man is separated from God and His love because of man's sin. The Bible says, "All of us like sheep have gone astray, each of us has turned to his own way; but the LORD has caused the iniquity of us all to fall on Him" (Isaiah 53:6). Romans 3:23 says, "All have sinned and fall short of the glory of God." You may be thinking that "all" doesn't include you, but Psalm 14 tells us that God looked to and fro throughout the land to see if there was anyone who did good, and He found no one. "All" means *everyone,* including you and me. We are all separated from God. This leads us to principle 2.

Principle 2: We owe a penalty for our sin. Hebrews 9:27 says that man is destined to die once and after this comes judgment. Second Thessalonians 1:8-9 says, "[The Lord Jesus] will punish those who do not know God and do not obey the gospel of our Lord Jesus. They will be punished with everlasting destruction and shut out from the presence of the Lord" (NIV).

Our sin has separated us from God, and we will be judged for our sin. We owe a penalty for our sinfulness that must be paid. The problem is that we're not worthy to pay that penalty. No amount of good works can put us back in right standing with God. There is a solution, however!

Principle 3: Christ paid the penalty for our sins. Romans 5:8 says, "God demonstrates His own love toward us, in that while we were yet sinners, Christ died for us." First Peter 3:18 says, "Christ also died for sins once for all, the just for the unjust, so that He might bring us to God, having been put to death in the flesh, but made alive in the spirit."

Jesus Christ came to earth and was born of a virgin to die on the cross to pay the penalty for your sins and mine. He rose again, signifying the penalty had been paid and accepted by God. But it's not enough just to believe the first three principles. We must go on to the next one.

Principle 4: We must individually accept Christ's payment for our sins. We can believe that Christ died for our sins, but if we never appropriate or accept that payment for our sins through faith we will perish in our sins. Only those who personally receive Jesus Christ into their lives, trusting Him to forgive their sins by faith, can be put in right standing with God and receive the power that only He can give. John 1:12 says, "As many as received Him, to them He gave the right to become children of God, even to those who believe in His name." John 5:24 says, "Truly, truly, I say to you, he who hears My word, and believes Him who sent Me, has eternal life, and does not come into judgment, but has passed out of death into life."

How can a person appropriate the reality of Jesus Christ into his or her life? Very simply, he or she does that *by faith.* Jesus said, "Behold, I stand at the door and knock; if anyone hears My voice and opens the door, I will come in to him and will dine with him, and he with Me" (Revelation 3:20). God is knocking on the door of your life! To invite Him in, all you need to do is pray a simple prayer that expresses the desire of your heart to turn away from sin, accept His gift of salvation, and make Jesus the Lord of your life. If you'd like, you can use this prayer or something similar:

> Lord Jesus, please come into my life and be my Savior and Lord. You said You'd forgive my sins and give me the gift of eternal life if I ask. I believe You! Thank You for paying for my sins and defeating Satan through Your death on the cross and Your resurrection.

This prayer, if it expresses the desire of your heart, opens the door of your heart and allows Christ to come into your life. He won't enter without your invitation. After you accept His gift, you can know He is with you because the Bible says so! "And the testimony is this, that God has given us eternal life, and this life is in His Son. He who has the Son has the life; he who does not have the Son of God does not have the life. These things I have written to you who believe in the name of the Son of God, so that you may know that you have eternal life" (1 John 5:11-13).

May God bless you and encourage you as you pursue your life in Christ and harmony in your marriage.

Recommended Resources

Books

Alcorn, Randy. *Money, Possessions, & Eternity.* Carol Stream, IL: Tyndale House Publishers, 2003.

Allender, Dan B., and Tremper Longman III. *Intimate Allies.* Wheaton, IL: Tyndale House Publishers, 1999.

Blue, Ron. *The New Master Your Money.* Chicago: Moody Publishers, 2004.

Blue, Ron, and Judy Blue. *Your Kids Can Master Their Money.* Wheaton, IL: Tyndale House Publishers, 2006.

Chapell, Bryan, and Kathy Chapell. *Each for the Other.* Grand Rapids, MI: Baker Books, 2006.

Chapman, Gary. *The Five Love Languages.* Chicago: Northfield Publishing, 2009.

Cooper, Darien. *You Can Be the Wife of a Happy Husband.* Shippensburg, PA: Destiny Image Publishers, 2011.

Dobson, James. *Love for a Lifetime.* Portland, OR: Multnomah Publishers, 2004.

Gilder, George. *Men and Marriage.* Gretna, LA: Pelican Publishing Co., 1992.

LaHaye, Tim. *Spirit-Controlled Temperament.* Wheaton, IL: Tyndale House Publishers, 1994.

Lewis, Robert, and William Hendricks. *Rocking the Roles*. Colorado Springs: NavPress, 1999.

Mason, Mike. *The Mystery of Marriage*. Portland, OR: Multnomah Press, 2005.

McGuire, Dorothy, Carol Lewis, and Alvena Blatchley. *Submission: Are There Limits?* Tri-R Associates, 1992. Tri-R Associates, PO Box 27567, Denver, CO 80227, www.tri-r-ministries.com, 303-989-6938.

Meredith, Don, and Sally Meredith. *2 Becoming One*. Chicago: Moody Press, 1999.

Packer, J.I. *Knowing God*. Downers Grove, IL: InterVarsity Press, 1993.

Parrott, Les, and Leslie Parrott. *Saving Your Marriage Before It Starts*. Grand Rapids, MI: Zondervan, 2006.

Ramsey, Dave. *The Total Money Makeover*. Nashville: Thomas Nelson Publishers, 2009.

Ryken, Leland. *Work and Leisure in Christian Perspective*. Eugene, OR: Wipf & Stock Publishers, 2002.

Smalley, Gary. *For Better or for Best*. Grand Rapids, MI: Zondervan, 2012.

___. *If Only He Knew*. Grand Rapids, MI: Zondervan, 2012.

Thomas, W. Ian. *Saving Life of Christ*. Grand Rapids, MI: Zondervan, 1961.

Wheat, Ed, and Gaye Wheat. *Intended for Pleasure*. Old Tappan, NJ: Revell, 2010.

Tape Series

The following tape series are available through Tri-R Associates, PO Box 27567, Denver, CO 80227, www.tri-r-ministries.com, 303-989-6938.

- "The Challenge of Christian Manhood."
- "The Challenge of Christian Womanhood."
- "Focusing on Christian Womanhood."

Living Expenses Worksheet

Year: _____

	Paid Monthly	Paid Annually	Total Annual Amount
Housing:			
Mortgage/rent	_____	_____	_____
Insurance	_____	_____	_____
Property taxes	_____	_____	_____
Electricity	_____	_____	_____
Heating	_____	_____	_____
Water	_____	_____	_____
Sanitation	_____	_____	_____
Telephone	_____	_____	_____
Cleaning	_____	_____	_____
Repairs and maintenance	_____	_____	_____
Supplies	_____	_____	_____
Improvements	_____	_____	_____
Furnishings	_____	_____	_____
Total housing	_____	_____	_____
Food	_____	_____	_____
Clothing (Annual)	_____	_____	_____
Transportation: (not paid by corp. if applicable)			
Insurance	_____	_____	_____
Gas and oil	_____	_____	_____
Maintenance and repairs (Annual)	_____	_____	_____
Parking	_____	_____	_____
Other	_____	_____	_____
Total transportation	_____	_____	_____
Entertainment and Recreation:			
Eating out	_____	_____	_____
Babysitters	_____	_____	_____
Magazines and newspapers	_____	_____	_____
Vacation (Annual)	_____	_____	_____
Clubs and activities	_____	_____	_____
Total entertainment and recreation	_____	_____	_____

Medical Expenses:
Insurance _____ _____ _____
Doctors _____ _____ _____
Dentists _____ _____ _____
Drugs _____ _____ _____
Other _____ _____ _____
  Total medical (Annual) _____ _____ _____

Insurance:
Life _____ _____ _____
Disability _____ _____ _____
  Total insurance _____ _____ _____

Children:
School lunches _____ _____ _____
Allowances _____ _____ _____
Tuition (grade & high school) _____ _____ _____
Tuition (college) _____ _____ _____
Lessons _____ _____ _____
Other _____ _____ _____
  Total children _____ _____ _____

Gifts:
Christmas _____ _____ _____
Birthdays _____ _____ _____
Anniversary _____ _____ _____
Other _____ _____ _____
  Total gifts (Annual) _____ _____ _____

Miscellaneous:
Toiletries _____ _____ _____
Husband lunches & miscellaneous _____ _____ _____
Wife miscellaneous _____ _____ _____
Dry cleaning _____ _____ _____
Animals (license, food, veterinarian) _____ _____ _____
Beauty and barber _____ _____ _____
_____ _____ _____ _____
_____ _____ _____ _____
  Total miscellaneous _____ _____ _____
  Total living expenses $_____ $_____ $_____

Notes

Introduction

1. W. Bradford Wilcox, *The State of Our Unions: Marriage in America 2009*, The National Marriage Project and the Center for Marriage and Families at the Institute for American Values, University of Virginia, PO Box 400766, Charlottesville, VA, 22904, 27-28.

Chapter 1: The Purpose of Money

1. Bill Gillham, *Lifetime Guarantee* (Brentwood, TN: Woglemuth & Hyatt, 1987), 76-77.

2. Major W. Ian Thomas, *The Saving Life of Christ* (Grand Rapids, MI: Zondervan Publishing House, 1961), 70-71.

3. Philip Yancey, "Learning to Live with Money," *Christianity Today*, December 14, 1984.

4. Randy Alcorn, *Money, Possessions, & Eternity* (Carol Stream, IL: Tyndale House, 2003), 42.

Chapter 2: The Purpose of Marriage

1. Mike Mason, *The Mystery of Marriage* (Portland, OR: Multnomah, 1985), 139.

2. Bryan Chapell, *Each for the Other* (Grand Rapids, MI: Baker Books, 1998), 97.

3. Mason, *Mystery of Marriage*, 101.

4. Cited in George Gilder, *Men and Marriage* (Gretna, LA: Pelican, 1986), 43.

5. James Dobson, *Straight Talk to Men and Their Wives* (Waco, TX: Word Books, 1980), 64.

6. Dan B. Allender and Tremper Longman III, *Intimate Allies* (Wheaton, IL: Tyndale House, 1995), 144.

7. *Common Ground*, 1987, Search Ministries, PO Box 521, Lutherville, MD 21093.

Chapter 3: Reasons for Marriage Conflict

1. James Dobson, *Love for a Lifetime* (Portland, OR: Multnomah, 1987), 70.

2. David Wills, Terry Parker, Greg Sperry, *Family. Money.*, National Christian Foundation, 2008, 12-13, 11625 Rainwater Drive, Suite 500, Alpharetta, GA, 30009.

3. Tim LaHaye, *Spirit-Controlled Temperament* (Wheaton, IL: Tyndale House, 1966), 5-6.

4. Gary Smalley, *If Only He Knew* (King of Prussia, PA: R.M. Marketing, 1979), 5.

5. Mike Mason, *The Mystery of Marriage* (Portland, OR: Multnomah, 1985), 129.

6. Dobson, *Love for a Lifetime*, 44.

7. *Myers-Briggs:* http://www.myersbriggsreports.com/?pn=Myers%2DBriggs +Type+Indicator+%2D+Overview+Profile+Report&p=743&c=27;__*DISC:* http://www.onlinediscprofile.com/discclassic.html?gclid=CM3U89a4mqs CFRFR7Aod00nEjQ; *RightPath:* http://www.rightpath.com/products/default.asp; *StrengthsFinder:* http://www.strengthsfinder.com/home.aspx.

Chapter 4: Work: Blessing or Curse?

1. Charles F. Deems, "The Study," 1879, quoted in Charles Spurgeon, *The Treasury of David*, vol. 3 (Part 2), Psalm 127, under "Explanatory Notes and Quaint Sayings," verse 2, accessed August 3, 2011, www.spurgeon.org/treasury/ps127.htm.

Chapter 5: Will He Ever Come Home?

1. Gordon MacDonald, *The Effective Father* (Wheaton, IL: Tyndale House, 1983), 35, 44, 50-51.

2. Tim Hansel, *What Kids Need Most in a Dad* (Old Tappan, NJ: Fleming H. Revell, 1984), 30, 165, 28.

Chapter 6: The Myth of the Working Mother

1. Survey conducted by Afterschool Alliance and JC Penney Afterschool, Oct. 2009, http://www.afterschoolalliance.org/AA3PM.cfm, accessed July 5, 2012.

2. "Weathering the Stress," *The Atlanta Journal and Constitution*, November 15, 1988.

3. George Gilder, *Men and Marriage* (Gretna, LA: Pelican, 1986), 153.

4. Robert Lewis and William Hendricks, *Rocking the Roles* (Colorado Springs: NavPress, 1991), 96-97.

5. Gilder, *Men and Marriage*, 44.

6. W. Bradford Wilcox, *The State of Our Unions: Marriage in America 2009*,

The National Marriage Project and the Center for Marriage and Families at the Institute for American Values, University of Virginia, PO Box 400766, Charlottesville, VA, 22904, 19.

7. Gilder, *Men and Marriage,* 151-52.

8. Ibid., 152-53.

9. Ibid., 153.

10. "Children of Change," *Atlanta Journal,* November 16, 1988.

11. Ibid.

12. Gilder, *Men and Marriage,* 154.

13. Jack Wilkinson, "Nothing Is Forgotten in Dr. Denmark's Office," *Atlanta Constitution,* April 1, 1986.

Chapter 8: Freedom in Control

1. For an online envelope system, check out MVelopes, http://www.mvel opes.com.

Chapter 9: The Banker Is Calling

1. Dave Ramsey, *The Total Money Makeover* (Nashville: Thomas Nelson, 2007), 19.

Chapter 10: But It's Such a Good Deal!

1. C.A. Stevens, "Women Are Something Else!" *Frontier Magazine,* 1982.

2. Ronald W. Blue, *Master Your Money* (Nashville: Thomas Nelson, 1986), 180-81.

Chapter 13: A Woman's Perspective on Her God-Given Roles

1. Matthew Henry, *Commentary on the Whole Bible,* ed. L.F. Church (Grand Rapids, MI: Zondervan, 1961), 788.

2. George Santa, *A Modern Study in the Book of Proverbs* (Milford, MI: Mott, 1978), 733.

3. Sam L. Peoples, Jr., *A Stress Management Seminar* (Birmingham: Christian Ministries, ND), 2.

4. Dave Ramsey, *The Total Money Makeover* (Nashville: Thomas Nelson, 2009), 31.

5. Major Ian Thomas, *The Saving Life of Christ* (Grand Rapids, MI: Zondervan, 1976), 15.

6. Major Ian Thomas, *The Mystery of Godliness* (Grand Rapids, MI: Zondervan, 1964), 47.

About the Author

 **Russ Crosson** is president and CEO of Ronald Blue & Co, LLC, one of the largest independent, fee-only financial, investment, tax, estate, and philanthropic advisory firms in the United States. With a national network of 15 branch offices, the firm serves more than 6,500 individual and business clients. Russ graduated from Kansas State University with a BS in mathematics and an MA in education. He and his wife, Julie, live in Georgia and are active in teaching and mentoring married couples. They are the parents of three adult sons.

Also available from Russ Crosson and Harvest House Publishers

Your Life...Well Spent

When most people think about money, they think about what money can do for them right now. But attitudes about money have an eternal aspect. Author and financial wizard Russ Crosson, CEO of Ronald Blue & Co. and a highly respected investment advisor, offers you a look at how to manage your money with eternity in view. You'll explore a new way of thinking about money, about your work, and about how to get a higher return on life. Topics covered include:

- a new understanding of work
- the four financial decisions that affect eternity
- raising children

You'll also examine the difference between prosperity and posterity, and uncover why one is more important than the other. Discover the freedom that comes when you approach your life and finances using the principles God shares in His Word.

The Truth About Money Lies

As long as we can make the payments, we're okay...aren't we? To answer this and other provocative questions relating to your money, financial expert Russ Crosson teams up with gifted communicator Kelly Talamo to expose the common lies people believe about money.

Through the use of everyday stories about men and women wrestling with financial decisions just like the ones we all make, Russ and Kelly refute these lies by revealing what the Bible says is the truth about money. Included are subtle lies that permeate our culture:

- We can't afford to give to our church or charity.
- What we do with our money is our own business.
- The more we have, the happier we'll be.

To learn more about books by Russ Crosson
or to read sample chapters, log on to our website:

www.HarvestHousePublishers.com

Ronald Blue&Co.
Wisdom for Wealth. For Life.

Corporate Profile

Ronald Blue & Co., LLC, is a national financial, estate, tax, and investment consulting firm serving clients through a network of 15 offices in the United States. Their professional services, based on biblical principles of financial management, include:

- Comprehensive, fee-only financial and estate planning
- Investment analysis and management
- Philanthropic counsel and strategies for charitable giving
- Tax preparation & business services for individuals and organizations
- Retirement plan services and fiduciary discharge

Headquartered in Atlanta, Georgia, Ronald Blue & Co. was founded in 1979 and employs more than 250 staff members. Serving over 5,000 individual and institutional clients, the firm manages approximately $6 billion in investment assets.

Our advisors have the training and experience to offer professional financial counsel and to assist clients in achieving their financial objectives.

The firm's founder, Ron Blue, has authored nine books on personal money management, including the bestseller *Master Your Money*. Russ Crosson, president/CEO, is an experienced author, speaker, and wealth transfer advisor.

Ronald Blue & Co. Branch Office Locations

Atlanta, GA	Kansas City, KS
Baltimore, MD	Montgomery, AL
Charlotte, NC	Nashville, TN
Chicago, IL	Orlando, FL
Fort Lauderdale, FL	Phoenix, AZ
Holland, MI	Santa Ana, CA
Houston, TX	Seattle, WA
Indianapolis, IN	

Contacting Ronald Blue & Co.

Internet: www.ronblue.com
Mail: 300 Colonial Center Parkway
Suite 300
Roswell, GA 30076

Phone: 1-800-841-0362
Fax: 770-280-6001
Email: info@ronblue.com